5. Klasse

Englisch Kurzgeschichten Mystery-Abenteuer durch London

Inkl.
Vokabeln, Grammatik, Übungen und über
40 Audios

Dr. Stefanie Fricke

1. Auflage April 2024

Ehrengut Verlag
c/o COCENTER GmbH
Koppoldstr. 1
86551 Aichach

www.ehrengut-verlag.de
info@ehrengut-verlag.de

Korrektorat: Jules Bold
Illustrator: Jeanne Lolness (Vy Bui)
Umschlaggestaltung: Jessica Scollo
Mitwirkende: Verena Schuster
Druck: CPI Druckdienstleistungen GmbH, Ferdinand-Jühlke-Straße 7, 99095 Erfurt

ISBN: 978-3-982523057

INHALT

INTRODUCTION – EINLEITUNG

Liebe Leserin, lieber Leser,

du hast häufig **keine Lust**, Englisch zu lernen? Englisch-Vokabeln und -Grammatik kannst du dir **nicht immer leicht merken**? Deine **Noten** könnten besser sein?
Oder suchst du nach einer **unterhaltsamen Möglichkeit**, den **Stoff der 5. Klasse zu wiederholen** und deine **Englischkenntnisse spielend einfach zu verbessern?** Wenn du dich angesprochen fühlst, ist das Buch genau richtig für dich!

Von Englisch-Didaktikerin und Schülern entwickelt

Zusammen mit meinen Kindern Sarah (12) und Markus (10) habe ich eine Abenteuergeschichte geschrieben, mit der du **ganz einfach deine Englischkenntnisse verbessern** kannst. Die zwei Hauptfiguren Mary und John werden dich auf eine spannende Reise durch London mitnehmen. Die **durchlaufende Handlung** ist auf 12 Kapitel aufgeteilt, in denen Sprache und Grammatik zunehmend anspruchsvoller werden.

Wie du mit dem Buch deine Englischkenntnisse verbesserst

Du kannst dir alle Texte **als Audio anhören**, so dass du gleichzeitig und **mühelos das Zuhören und Hörverstehen trainierst** und die **richtige Aussprache** verinnerlichst. Dabei ist es dir überlassen, ob du zuerst selbst den Text liest, und danach erst das Audio anhörst, ob du das Audio hörst und dabei mitliest, oder ob du nur das Audio anhörst und versuchst, auch ohne den geschriebenen Text die Geschichte zu verstehen (das ist am schwersten und auch am besten, um das Hörverständnis zu trainieren).

Lückentexte, Verständnisfragen und kurze Vokabel- und Grammatikübungen helfen dir, den Stoff der 5. Klasse zu wiederholen und zu festigen. Keine Sorge, falls du wirklich etwas nicht verstehen solltest! Am Ende eines jeden Kapitels findest du die **deutsche Übersetzung der Geschichte**. Nimm zur Bearbeitung der Übungen am besten Block und Stift, dann kannst du die Übungen gegebenenfalls mehrmals machen oder das Buch auch an Freunde und/oder Geschwister weiterreichen.

Zeitdruck gibt es nicht. Ob und wann du lesen, hören und üben willst, und wie viele Kapitel du auf einmal machst – **du bestimmst dein Tempo und deinen Lernstil. Die Entscheidung liegt ganz bei dir!**

Die Vokabeln und Grammatik in diesem Buch entsprechen dem **Lehrplan der 5. Klasse**. Also genau den Inhalten, die du auch in der Schule lernst. **Unbekannte Vokabeln kannst du leicht in der Vokabelliste finden.** Solltest du Erklärungen zur Grammatik benötigen, kannst du sie schnell und einfach in deinem Schulbuch nachlesen.

Du wirst sehen, dass du mit jedem Kapitel mehr verstehst. Und auch wenn du nicht jedes Wort weißt, ist das kein Problem: Versuche einfach, dir die Bedeutung aus dem Kontext zu erschließen.

Ich freue mich, dass du Mary und John auf ihrer Suche nach dem verlorenen Manuskript begleitest. Viel Freude beim Lesen, Hören und Üben!

Deine Stefanie Fricke

AUDIODATEIEN

Wir möchten, dass du zusätzlich zu deinem **Leseverständnis** auch **dein Hörverständnis** und **deine Aussprache verbesserst**. Deshalb findest du **über 40 Audiodateien** zu allen 12 Geschichten, Übungen und Vokabellisten **auf unserer Website** und **zum kostenlosen Download**. **Höre dir die Audioinhalte öfters an** und **sprich laut mit**, um ein **besseres Gefühl für den Klang** und die **Aussprache** der englischen Sprache zu bekommen. Wenn du das Gefühl hast, dass **zu schnell** gesprochen wird, dann **reguliere die Geschwindigkeit** einfach auf deinem Gerät.

Und so geht's:
Öffne die Kamera-App auf deinem Smartphone oder deinem Tablet und richte die Kamera auf den QR-Code. Wenn du eine gute Internetverbindung hast, öffnet sich das Zusatzmaterial ganz automatisch. Falls die Kamera-App auf deinem Smartphone die Funktion zum QR-Code scannen nicht hat, kannst du den Code alternativ auch mit einer **QR-Scanner-App** öffnen oder direkt auf unsere Website zugreifen (URL aus QR-Code):

https://www.ehrengut-verlag.de/audios/Englisch-Kurzgeschichten-5-Klasse

Bei Problemen schreibe uns gerne an **info@ehrengut-verlag.de.** Wir werden uns zeitnah bei dir melden und dir beim Lösen deines Problems helfen.

01 | MARY MEETS JOHN

Personal pronouns and forms of to be

Mary is 11 years old and lives in London. One day, Mary is walking in the park. After **crossing** a bridge over a small **creek**, she suddenly sees a dog. A golden retriever stands alone in the middle of the **path**. Mary walks towards him. She likes dogs.

"Hello, you," she says. "Are you alone? Where is your **owner**?"

The dog **licks** her hand and Mary **pets** him. She waits a few minutes, but no one comes. What can she do now? Suddenly, an idea comes to her. She looks at the dog's **collar** and finds a **pendant** with a phone number.

But Mary hasn't got a mobile phone. She looks around and sees a woman with a small dog. Mary takes the golden retriever by the collar, walks over to the woman and tells her that she has **found** the dog.

"Do you want to use my mobile phone?" the woman asks.

"Yes, please."

Mary **dials** the number. A man answers. "You found our dog, Mycroft? We are so happy! Where are you?"

Mary tells him, and he asks her to wait for him.

After a few minutes, Mary sees a man and a boy **about her age**.

They smile when they see her.

"Mycroft!" the boy shouts as he runs over to pet the dog. He turns to Mary. "Thank you so much! I'm John."

"Hi, I am Mary."

"Do you like Mycroft?" John asks.

"Yes, he's **lovely**!"

"If you want, we can meet here in the park and play with him."

Mary smiles. "Yes, that would be great."

Vocabulary

Englisch	Deutsch
to cross	überqueren
the creek	der Bach
the path	der Pfad
the owner	der Besitzer
to lick	lecken
to pet	streicheln
the collar	das Halsband
the pendant	der Anhänger
found	Vergangenheit von to find = finden
to dial	wählen
about her age	ungefähr in ihrem Alter
lovely	wunderbar, großartig

Gap text 1: Personal pronouns

Fill in personal pronouns (*I, you, he/she/it, we, you, they*)

Mary is 11 years old and lives in London. One day, Mary is walking in the park. After **crossing** a bridge over a small **creek**, (1) ______ suddenly sees a dog. A golden retriever stands alone in the middle of the **path**. Mary walks towards him. (2) ______ likes dogs.

"Hello, you," she says. "Are (3) ______ alone? Where is your **owner**?"

The dog **licks** her hand and Mary **pets** him. She waits a few minutes, but no one comes. What can she do now? Suddenly, an idea comes to her. (4) ______ looks at the dog's **collar** and finds a **pendant** with a phone number.

But Mary hasn't got a mobile phone. She looks around and sees a woman with a small dog. Mary takes the golden retriever by the collar, walks over to the woman and tells her that she has **found** the dog.

"Do (5) ______ want to use my mobile phone?" the woman asks.

"Yes, please."

Mary **dials** the number. A man answers. "You found our dog, Mycroft? (6) ______ are so happy! Where are (7) ____?"

Mary tells him, and (8) ______ asks her to wait for him.

After a few minutes, Mary sees a man and a boy **about her age**. They smile when (9) ______ see her.

"Mycroft!" the boy shouts as he runs over to pet the dog. (10) ______ turns to Mary. "Thank you so much! I'm John."

"Hi, (11) ______ am Mary."

"Do (12) ______ like Mycroft?" John asks.

"Yes, he's **lovely**!"

"If you want, (13) ______ can meet here in the park and play with him."

Mary smiles. "Yes, that would be great."

Gap text 2: Forms of to be

Fill in forms of to be (*am, is, are*)

Mary (1) ______ 11 years old and lives in London. One day, Mary is walking in the park. After **crossing** a bridge over a small **creek**, she suddenly sees a dog. A golden retriever stands alone in the middle of the **path**. Mary walks towards him. She likes dogs.

"Hello, you," she says. "(2) ______ you alone? Where (3) ______ your **owner**?"

The dog **licks** her hand and Mary **pets** him. She waits a few minutes, but no one comes. What can she do now? Suddenly, an idea comes to her. She looks at the dog's **collar** and finds a **pendant** with a phone number.

But Mary hasn't got a mobile phone. She looks around and sees a woman with a small dog. Mary takes the golden retriever by the collar, walks over to the woman and tells her that she has **found** the dog.

"Do you want to use my mobile phone?" the woman asks.

"Yes, please."

Mary **dials** the number. A man answers. "You found our dog, Mycroft? We (4) ______ so happy! Where (5) ______ you?"

Mary tells him, and he asks her to wait for him.

After a few minutes, Mary sees a man and a boy **about her age**. They smile when they see her.

"Mycroft!" the boy shouts as he runs over to pet the dog. He turns to Mary. "Thank you so much! I'm John."

"Hi, I (6) ______ Mary."

"Do you like Mycroft?" John asks.

"Yes, he (7) ______ **lovely**!"

"If you want, we can meet here in the park and play with him."

Mary smiles. "Yes, that would be great."

Answer the questions about the story

(1) How old is Mary?
(2) Where does Mary live?
(3) Where does she meet the dog?
(4) Where does Mary find the phone number?
(5) Why can't she phone the owner?
(6) What is the dog's name?

(1) ____

(2) ____

(3) ____

(4) ____

(5) ____

(6)____

Translation
MARY TRIFFT JOHN

Mary ist 11 Jahre alt und lebt in London. Eines Tages geht Mary im Park spazieren. Nachdem sie eine Brücke über einen kleinen Bach überquert hat, sieht sie plötzlich einen Hund. Ein Golden Retriever steht allein in der Mitte des Weges. Mary geht auf ihn zu. Sie mag Hunde.

„Hallo, du", sagt sie. „Bist du allein? Wo ist dein Besitzer?"

Der Hund leckt ihr die Hand und Mary streichelt ihn. Sie wartet ein paar Minuten, aber es kommt niemand. Was kann sie jetzt tun? Plötzlich kommt ihr eine Idee. Sie sieht sich das Halsband des Hundes an und findet einen Anhänger mit einer Telefonnummer.

Aber Mary hat kein Handy. Sie schaut sich um und sieht eine Frau mit einem kleinen Hund. Mary nimmt den Golden Retriever am Halsband, geht zu der Frau hinüber und sagt ihr, dass sie einen Hund gefunden hat.

„Willst du mein Handy benutzen?", fragt die Frau.

„Ja, bitte."

Mary wählt die Nummer. Ein Mann meldet sich. „Du hast unseren Hund Mycroft gefunden? Wir sind so glücklich! Wo bist du?"

Mary sagt es ihm, und er bittet sie, auf ihn zu warten.

Nach ein paar Minuten sieht Mary einen Mann und einen Jungen in ihrem Alter. Sie lächeln, als sie sie sehen.

„Mycroft!", ruft der Junge und rennt hinüber, um den Hund zu streicheln. Er wendet sich zu Mary. „Vielen Dank! Ich bin John."

„Hallo, ich bin Mary."

„Magst du Mycroft?" Fragt John.

„Ja, er ist großartig!"

„Wenn du willst, können wir uns hier im Park treffen und mit ihm spielen."

Mary lächelt. „Ja, das wäre toll."

02 | AT THE FLEA MARKET

The possessive form with 's and of-genitive and possessive adjectives

Mary and John **quickly** become friends. Their families live in the same part of London, and the two children often **spend their time** playing in the park with John's dog, Mycroft.

One day, there is a flea market at the **entrance** of the park.

"I love flea markets!" John says. "Have you got any money?"

Mary takes out her **purse**. "Yes, five pounds. Let's have a look."

There are long tables with many different things: clothes, books, toys, **paintings**, and **sports equipment**.

"Look, there's a picture of a dog who looks just like Mycroft!" Mary says.

"You're right. And look at the colour of that old bicycle over there, it's crazy," John says.

They walk through the flea market until John stops and looks at some books. "These are Sherlock Holmes stories," he tells Mary. "He is my favourite **detective**."

"Who is the author of the stories?"

"Conan Doyle."

"Is he your favourite author?"

"Yes. That's also where Mycroft has got his name from. 'Mycroft' is the name of Sherlock Holmes's brother."

As John **leaves through several** books, a few pieces of paper suddenly fall out of one. He picks them up, his eyes widening with excitement. "Do you know what this is?" John asks.

Mary sees only **drawings** of little dancing **match stick men**. "No idea."

"It's a **cypher**. I know it from one of Conan Doyle's stories."

"Do you think this is a **secret** message?"

John looks at the book and the pieces of paper with the strange drawings. "I don't know. But this is a really old book, and the pieces of paper look old too. Let's buy the book, go to my house, and see if I can **decipher** the code."

Vocabulary

Englisch	Deutsch
the flea market	der Flohmarkt
quickly	schnell
to spend time	Zeit verbringen
the entrance	der Eingang
the purse	der Geldbeutel
the painting	das Gemälde
the sports equipment	die Sportgeräte
the detective	der Dedektiv
to leave through	durchblättern

several	einige, verschiedene
the drawing	die Zeichnung
the match stick man	das Strichmännchen
the cypher	die Geheimschrift, der Code
secret	geheim
to decipher	entziffern

Gap text 1: Possessive forms

Fill in possessive forms with *'s* and *of-genitive*

Mary and John **quickly** become friends. Their families live in the same part (1) ______ London, and the two children often **spend their time** playing in the park with John (2) ______ dog, Mycroft.

One day, there is a flea market at the **entrance** (3) ______ the park.

"I love flea markets!" John says. "Have you got any money?"

Mary takes out her **purse**. "Yes, five pounds. Let's have a look."

There are long tables with many different things: clothes, books, toys, **paintings**, and sports equipment.

"Look, there's a picture (4) ______ a dog who looks just like Mycroft!" Mary says.

"You're right. And look at the colour (5) ______ that old bicycle over there, it's crazy," John says.

They walk through the flea market until John stops and looks at some books. "These are Sherlock Holmes stories," he tells Mary. "He is my favourite **detective**."

"Who is the author (6) ______ the stories?"

"Conan Doyle."

"Is he your favourite author?"

"Yes. That's also where Mycroft has got his name from.

'Mycroft' is the name of Sherlock Holmes (7) ______ brother."

As John **leaves through several** books, a few pieces of paper suddenly fall out of one. He picks them up, his eyes widening with excitement. "Do you know what this is?" John asks.

Mary sees only **drawings** of little dancing **match stick men**. "No idea."

"It's a **cypher**. I know it from one of Conan Doyle (8) ______ stories."

"Do you think this is a **secret** message?"

John looks at the book and the pieces of paper with the strange drawings. "I don't know. But this is a really old book, and the pieces of paper look old too. Let's buy the book, go to my house, and see if I can **decipher** the code."

Gap text 2: Possessive adjectives

Fill in possessive adjectives *(my, your, his/her/its, our, their)*

Mary and John **quickly** become friends. (1) ______ families live in the same part of London, and the two children often **spend** (2) ______ **time** playing in the park with John's dog, Mycroft.

One day, there is a flea market at the **entrance** of the park.

"I love flea markets!" John says. "Have you got any money?"

Mary takes out (3) ______ **purse**. "Yes, five pounds. Let's have a look."

There are long tables with many different things: clothes, books, toys, **paintings**, and **sports equipment**.

"Look, there's a picture of a dog who looks just like Mycroft!" Mary says.

"You're right. And look at the colour of that old bicycle over there, it's crazy," John says.

They walk through the flea market until John stops and looks at some books. "These are Sherlock Holmes stories," he tells Mary.

"He is (4) ______ favourite **detective**."

"Who is the author of the stories?"

"Conan Doyle."

"Is he (5) ______ favourite author?"

"Yes. That's also where Mycroft has got (6) ______ name from. 'Mycroft' is the name of Sherlock Holmes's brother."

As John **leaves through several** books, a few pieces of paper suddenly fall out of one. He picks them up, (7) ______ eyes widening with excitement. "Do you know what this is?" John asks.

Mary sees only **drawings** of little dancing **match stick men**. "No idea."

"It's a **cypher**. I know it from one of Conan Doyle's stories."

"Do you think this is a **secret** message?"

John looks at the book and the pieces of paper with the strange drawings. "I don't know. But this is a really old book, and the pieces of paper look old too. Let's buy the book, go to (8) ______ house, and see if I can **decipher** the code."

Complete the sentences using the possessive adjectives *my, your, his/her/its, our, their*

(1) John has got a dog. It's ______ dog.
(2) I have got a sister. She's ______ sister.
(3) My brother and I have got a computer. It's ______ computer.
(4) You have got a bike. This is ______ bike.
(5) She has got a brother. He's ______ brother.
(6) My parents have got a car. It's ______ car.
(7) This bike is red. Red is ______ colour.

Translation
AUF DEM FLOHMARKT

Mary und John werden schnell Freunde. Ihre Familien leben im selben Stadtteil Londons, und die beiden Kinder verbringen ihre Zeit oft im Park, wo sie mit Johns Hund Mycroft spielen.

Eines Tages findet am Eingang des Parks ein Flohmarkt statt.

„Ich liebe Flohmärkte!“ sagt John. „Hast du Geld dabei?“

Mary holt ihr Portemonnaie heraus. „Ja, fünf Pfund. Schauen wir uns um.“

Es gibt lange Tische mit vielen verschiedenen Dingen: Kleidung, Bücher, Spielzeug, Bilder und Sportgeräte.

„Sieh mal, da ist ein Bild von einem Hund, der genauso aussieht wie Mycroft!“ sagt Mary.

„Du hast recht. Und sieh dir die Farbe des alten Fahrrads dort drüben an, das ist verrückt“, sagt John.

Sie gehen durch den Flohmarkt, bis John stehen bleibt und sich einige Bücher ansieht. „Das sind Sherlock-Holmes-Geschichten“, sagt er zu Mary. „Er ist mein Lieblingsdetektiv.“

„Wer ist der Autor der Geschichten?“

„Conan Doyle.“

„Ist er dein Lieblingsautor?“

„Ja. Von ihm hat Mycroft auch seinen Namen. ‚Mycroft‘ ist der Name des Bruders von Sherlock Holmes.“

Als John in mehreren Büchern blättert, fallen plötzlich ein paar Zettel aus einem heraus. Er hebt sie auf und seine Augen weiten sich vor Aufregung. „Weißt du, was das ist?“ fragt John.

Mary sieht nur Zeichnungen von kleinen tanzenden Strichmännchen. „Keine Ahnung.“

„Es ist eine Geheimschrift. Ich kenne sie aus einer der Geschichten von Conan Doyle.“

„Meinst du, das ist eine geheime Botschaft?“

John sieht sich das Buch und die Zettel mit den seltsamen Zeichnungen an. „Ich weiß es nicht. Aber das ist ein wirklich altes

Buch, und die Zettel sehen auch alt aus. Lass uns das Buch kaufen, zu mir nach Hause gehen und sehen, ob ich die Geheimschrift entziffern kann.“

03 | THE LOST MANUSCRIPT

The plural: a, an, the

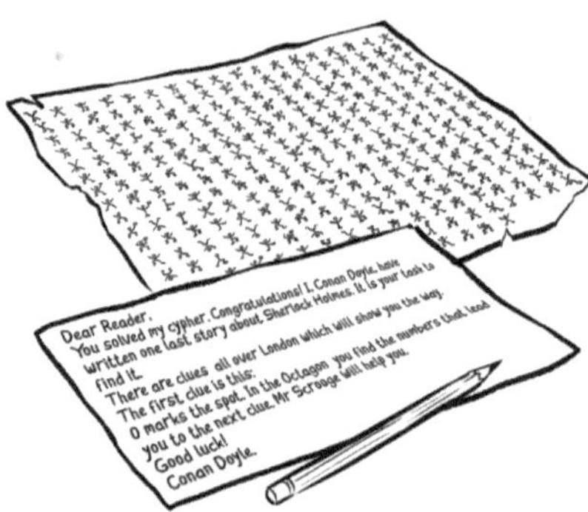

They buy the book and walk back to John's house. It's an old house, and John has got a large bedroom with a lot of books. John **searches through** them until he finds the Sherlock Holmes story with the dancing men **cypher**.

He starts **deciphering** the code and becomes more and more excited. When he is finished, he gives Mary the translation. "Look, it's a secret **letter** from Conan Doyle!"

London, 5 January 1929

Dear Reader,
You **solved** my cypher. Congratulations! I, Conan Doyle, have written one last story about Sherlock Holmes. It is your task to find the manuscript.
There are **clues** at four **locations** all around London. These clues, together with the clues on these papers, will show you the way.
The first clue is this:

0 ***marks*** *the* ***spot.*** *In the* ***Octagon*** *you find the numbers that show you the second location. There, Mr Scrooge will help you.*

Good luck!
Conan Doyle.

Mary looks at John. "Do you know anything about this manuscript?"

"There are **rumours** about it, but no one knows where it is. It would be so cool if we could find it!"

"But what does the clue mean?"

They both look at the paper.

Suddenly, Mary shouts, "I think I know it! It says, '*0 marks the spot.*' That could be the **prime meridian** at the **Royal Observatory** in Greenwich. I know it from a school trip."

"But what is the 'Octagon'?"

"I don't know, but **perhaps** we find it when we get to Greenwich."

"And who is Mr Scrooge?" John asks.

"The name sounds **familiar**...Perhaps he is an important person? Let's search on the internet."

They **type** in the name and find many results.

"Oh, I remember," Mary says, "it's a **character** from **Charles Dickens's** story *A Christmas Carol.* But what does that mean?"

"No idea, but perhaps it will make sense when we know where to go."

"What are the other clues?"

John hands her a second piece of paper. Mary reads:

Clue to find the third location: 1=15, 2=4, 3=9, 4=20, 5=35, 6=7, 7=2, 8=M, 9=26, 10=14, 11=6, 12=42, 13=M 14=17, 15=16, 16=7, 17=12, 18=39, 19=39, 20=3.

Clue to find the fourth location: ***folded cloth*** *–* ***quail chick****– quail chick*

Clue to find the fourth location: kauri 4 ***yards*** *up*

Clue to find the manuscript: YC.1929.S.25

"I hope this will all make sense when we find the right locations," John says.

"Yes, I hope so too. But don't worry about that now; at least we know where to go first."

Vocabulary

Englisch	Deutsch
lost	Vergangenheit von to lose: verlieren
the manuscript	das Manuskript
to search through	durchsuchen
the cypher	die Geheimschrift, der Code
to decipher	entziffern/entschlüsseln
the letter	der Brief
solved	Vergangenheit von to solve: lösen
the clue	der Hinweis
the location	der Ort, der Platz
to mark	markieren

the spot	der Ort, die Stelle
the octagon	das Achteck
the rumour	das Gerücht
the prime meridian	der Nullmeridian
the Royal Observatory	Das Observatorium in Greenwich (London) war ursprünglich das Observatorium für den königlichen Hofastronomen. Heute ist es ein Museum.
perhaps	vielleicht
familiar	bekannt
to type	tippen, schreiben
the character	die Figur, der Charakter
Charles Dickens	Berühmter englischer Schriftsteller (1812-1870). A Christmas Carol (Eine Weihnachtsgeschichte) von 1843 ist eines seiner bekanntesten Werke.
folded	Vergangenheit von to fold: falten
the cloth	der Stoff, das Tuch
the quail chick	das Wachtelküken
the yard	britisches Langenmaß (1 yard = 0,9144 m)

Gap text 1: Singular/plural forms and articles

Fill in *singular* or *plural forms* and *articles a, an, the*

They buy the book and walk back to John's house. It's (1) ______ (a/an/the) old house, and John has got a large bedroom with a lot of (2) ______ (book/books). John **searches through** them until he finds the Sherlock Holmes story with (3) ______ (a/an/the) dancing men **cypher**.

He starts **deciphering** the code and becomes more and more excited. When he is finished, he gives Mary the translation. "Look, it's (4) ______ (a/an/the) secret **letter** from Conan Doyle!"

London, 5 January 1929

Dear Reader,
You **solved** my cypher. Congratulations! I, Conan Doyle, have written one last story about Sherlock Holmes. It is your task to find (5) ______ (a/an/the) manuscript.
There are **clues** at four **locations** all around London. These (6) ______ (clue/clues), together with the clues on these papers, will show you the way.
The first (7) ______ (clue/clues) is this:

> *0 **marks** the **spot**. In the **Octagon** you find the numbers that show you the second location. There, Mr Scrooge will help you.*

Good luck!
Conan Doyle.

Mary looks at John. "Do you know anything about this (8) ______ (manuscript/manuscripts)?"

"There are **rumours** about it, but no one knows where it is. It would be so cool if we could find it!"

"But what does (9) ______ (a/an/the) clue mean?"

They both look at the paper.

Suddenly, Mary shouts, "I think I know it! It says, '*0 marks the spot.*' That could be the prime **meridian** at the **Royal Observatory** in Greenwich. I know it from (10) ______ (a/an/the) school trip."

"But what is the 'Octagon'?"

"I don't know, but **perhaps** we find it when we get to Greenwich."

"And who is Mr Scrooge?" John asks.

"The name sounds **familiar**...Perhaps he is (11) ______ (a/an/the) important person? Let's search on the internet."

They **type** in the name and find many results.

"Oh, I remember," Mary says, "it's a **character** from **Charles Dickens's** story *A Christmas Carol.* But what does that mean?"

"No idea, but perhaps it will make sense when we know where to go."

"What are the other clues?"

John hands her a second piece of paper. Mary reads:

Clue to find the third location: 1=15, 2=4, 3=9, 4=20, 5=35, 6=7, 7=2, 8=M, 9=26, 10=14, 11=6, 12=42, 13=M 14=17, 15=16, 16=7, 17=12, 18=39, 19=39, 20=3.

Clue to find the fourth location: ***folded cloth – quail chick*** *– quail chick*

Clue to find the fourth location: kauri 4 ***yards*** *up*

Clue to find the manuscript: YC.1929.S.25

"I hope this will all make sense when we find (12) ______ (a/an/the) right locations," John says.

"Yes, I hope so too. But don't worry about that now; at least we know where to go first."

Fill in the missing words

(1) John and Mary buy the book and walk back to John's ______.
(2) When John deciphers the code, he finds out that it is a secret ______ from Conan Doyle.
(3) Mr Scrooge is a character from Charles Dickens's ______ *A Christmas Carol*

Answer the questions about the story

(1) How can Mary and John find the manuscript?
(2) What does "0 marks the spot" mean?
(3) Who finds out what the first clue means?
(4) Who is the author of *A Christmas Carol*?

(1) ____

(2) ____

(3) ____

(4) ____

Translation
DAS VERLORENE MANUSKRIPT

Sie kaufen das Buch und gehen zurück zu Johns Haus. Es ist ein altes Haus, und John hat ein großes Schlafzimmer mit einer Menge Bücher. John durchsucht sie, bis er die Sherlock-Holmes-Geschichte mit der Geheimschrift der tanzenden Strichmännchen findet.

Er beginnt, den Code zu entziffern und wird immer aufgeregter. Als er fertig ist, gibt er Mary die Übersetzung. „Schau, ein geheimer Brief von Conan Doyle!"

London, 5. Januar 1929

Lieber Leser,

Sie haben meine Geheimschrift entziffert. Herzlichen Glückwunsch! Ich, Conan Doyle, habe eine letzte Geschichte über Sherlock Holmes geschrieben. Es ist Ihre Aufgabe, das Manuskript zu finden.

Es gibt Hinweise an vier Orten in ganz London. Diese Hinweise, zusammen mit den Hinweisen auf diesen Seiten, werden Ihnen den Weg weisen.

Der erste Hinweis ist:

0 markiert die Stelle. Im Oktagon finden Sie die Zahlen, die Sie zum zweiten Ort führen. Dort wird Ihnen Mr. Scrooge helfen.

Viel Glück!

Conan Doyle.

Mary sieht John an. „Weißt du etwas über dieses Manuskript?"

„Es gibt Gerüchte darüber, aber niemand weiß, wo es ist. Es wäre so cool, wenn wir es finden könnten!"

„Aber was bedeutet der Hinweis?"

Sie blicken beide auf das Papier.

Plötzlich ruft Mary: „Ich glaube, ich weiß es! Da steht: *‚0 markiert die Stelle'*. Das könnte der Nullmeridian beim Königlichen

Observatorium in Greenwich sein. Ich kenne ihn von einem Schulausflug."

„Aber was ist das ‚Oktagon'?"

„Ich weiß es nicht, aber vielleicht finden wir es, wenn wir in Greenwich sind."

„Und wer ist Mr. Scrooge?" fragt John.

„Der Name kommt mir bekannt vor... Vielleicht ist er eine wichtige Person? Lass uns im Internet suchen."

Sie geben den Namen ein und finden viele Ergebnisse.

„Oh, ich erinnere mich", sagt Mary, „es ist eine Figur aus Charles Dickens' Erzählung *Eine Weihnachtsgeschichte*. Aber was hat das zu bedeuten?"

„Keine Ahnung, aber vielleicht ergibt es einen Sinn, wenn wir wissen, wohin wir müssen."

„Was sind die anderen Hinweise?"

John reicht ihr einen zweiten Zettel. Mary liest:

> *Hinweis, um den dritten Ort zu finden: 1=15, 2=4, 3=9, 4=20, 5=35, 6=7, 7=2, 8=M, 9=26, 10=14, 11=6, 12=42, 13=M 14=17, 15=16, 16=7, 17=12, 18=39, 19=39, 20=3.*
>
> *Hinweis, um den vierten Ort zu finden: gefaltetes Tuch - Wachtelküken - Wachtelküken*
>
> *Hinweis, um den fünften Ort zu finden: Kauri 4 Yards oben*
>
> *Hinweis, um das Manuskript zu finden: YC.1929.S.25*

„Ich hoffe, dass das alles einen Sinn ergibt, wenn wir die richtigen Orte gefunden haben", sagt John.

„Ja, das hoffe ich auch. Aber mach dir darüber jetzt keine Sorgen; wenigstens wissen wir, wo wir zuerst hinmüssen."

04 | A BIG MISTAKE

Have and has got

"Then let's go to Greenwich!" Mary says.

"No, I have another idea," John replies. "I want to talk to an expert first. His name is Mr Milverton. I know him from the Sherlock Holmes fan club. He has got an **antique shop** at Russell Square."

"Then let's go!"

Mary and John walk to the nearest **tube station**.

"Have you got a ticket for the tube?" Mary asks John.

"No, I haven't got one. What about you?"

"I have got a ticket. Look, over there is a ticket machine."

They buy a ticket for John and then take the tube to Russell Square. John leads Mary to a small shop. A bell rings when they open the door. They see a man standing behind a desk. He is about 50 years old, thin and tall. He has short, dark hair, **piercing** blue eyes and a large nose.

As soon as he sees the man, Mycroft starts to **growl**.

"Sh, Mycroft," John says, and slowly, the dog stops.

"Hello, Mr Milverton," John says. "My name is John; you know me from the Sherlock Holmes fan club. This is my friend Mary."

"Hello, John. How can I help you?"

"We **found** this book at a flea market." John shows him the book. "And inside, we found this." He gives him the pieces of paper with the cypher.

Mr Milverton looks very interested. "This is the dancing men cipher! Have you got a translation?"

"Yes. It's a letter from Conan Doyle." John gives him the first page of the translation but not the second page with the other clues.

Mr Milverton reads it. "Hm. I don't know. I think this is fake."

John is disappointed. "Are you sure?"

"Yes. But you can **leave** the letter here. I have got a lot of books about Conan Doyle and can see if I can find anything about this."

Mary thinks Mr Milverton looks very **eager** to **keep** the letter. "No, thank you," she says. "We want it back."

Mr Milverton looks **reluctant**, but Mary holds out her hand, and he gives her the letter.

"Thank you," Mary and John say and leave the shop.

Vocabulary

Englisch	Deutsch
the antique shop	der Antiquitätenladen
the tube station	die U-Bahn-Station; „tube" ist die Londoner U-Bahn
piercing	bohrend, stechend
to growl	knurren
found	Vergangenheit von

	to find: finden
to leave	lassen, verlassen
eager	begierig
to keep	behalten
reluctant	widerwillig, zögernd

Gap text 1: Have got and haven't got

Fill in *have got/has got* or *haven't got/hasn't got*

"Then let's go to Greenwich!" Mary says.

"No, I have another idea," John replies. "I want to talk to an expert first. His name is Mr Milverton. I know him from the Sherlock Holmes fan club. He (1) ______ an **antique shop** at Russell Square."

"Then let's go!"

Mary and John walk to the nearest **tube station**.

"(2)____ you ______ a ticket for the tube?" Mary asks John.

"No, I (3) ______ one. What about you?"

"I (4) ______ a ticket. Look, over there is a ticket machine."

They buy a ticket for John and then take the tube to Russell Square. John leads Mary to a small shop. A bell rings when they open the door. They see a man standing behind a desk. He is about 50 years old, thin and tall. He has short, dark hair, **piercing** blue eyes and a large nose.

As soon as he sees the man, Mycroft starts to **growl**.

"Sh, Mycroft," John says, and slowly, the dog stops.

"Hello, Mr Milverton," John says. "My name is John; you know me from the Sherlock Holmes fan club. This is my friend Mary."

"Hello, John. How can I help you?"

"We **found** this book at a flea market." John shows him the book. “And inside, we found this.” He gives him the pieces of paper with the cypher.

Mr Milverton looks very interested. “This is the dancing men cipher! (5) ______ you ______ a translation?”

“Yes. It’s a letter from Conan Doyle.” John gives him the first page of the translation but not the second page with the other clues.

Mr Milverton reads it. “Hm. I don’t know. I think this is fake.”

John is disappointed. “Are you sure?”

“Yes. But you can **leave** the letter here. I (6) ______ a lot of books about Conan Doyle and can see if I can find anything about this.”

Mary thinks Mr Milverton looks very **eager** to **keep** the letter. “No, thank you,” she says. “We want it back.”

Mr Milverton looks **reluctant**, but Mary holds out her hand, and he gives her the letter.

“Thank you,” Mary and John say and leave the shop.

Complete the sentences using *have got/has got* or *haven’t got/hasn’t got*

(1) John ______ a dog.
(2) John ______ a ticket for the tube.
(3) Mary and John ______ the translation of the secret letter.

Build questions with *have got/has got*

Example:
She has got a ticket for the tube. => Has she got a ticket for the tube?

(1) We have got a car.
(2) You have got a pencil.
(3) I have got a cat.
(4) They have got two sons.
(5) He has got a red bike.

(1) ____

(2) ____

(3) ____

(4) ____

(5) ____

Match the words with the correct translation

1) idea	a) Übersetzung
2) the tube	b) enttäuscht
3) ticket machine	c) Idee, Einfall, Gedanke
4) translation	d) Die Londoner U-Bahn (wörtlich: Röhre, Tunnel)
5) disappointed	e) Experte
6) expert	f) Fahrkartenautomat

Translation
EIN GROSSER FEHLER

„Dann lass uns nach Greenwich fahren!“ sagt Mary.

„Nein, ich habe eine andere Idee“, antwortet John. „Ich möchte zuerst mit einem Experten sprechen. Sein Name ist Mr. Milverton. Ich kenne ihn aus dem Sherlock-Holmes-Fanclub. Er hat ein Antiquitätengeschäft am Russell Square.“

„Dann lass uns gehen!“

Mary und John laufen zur nächsten U-Bahn-Station.

„Hast du eine Fahrkarte für die U-Bahn?“ fragt Mary John.

„Nein, ich habe keine. Was ist mit dir?“

„Ich habe eine Fahrkarte. Schau mal, da drüben ist ein Fahrkartenautomat.“

Sie kaufen eine Fahrkarte für John und fahren dann mit der U-Bahn zum Russell Square. John führt Mary zu einem kleinen Laden. Als sie die Tür öffnen, läutet eine Glocke. Sie sehen einen Mann hinter einem Tisch stehen. Er ist etwa 50 Jahre alt, schlank und groß. Er hat kurzes, dunkles Haar, stechend blaue Augen und eine große Nase.

Sobald er den Mann sieht, beginnt Mycroft zu knurren.

„Pst, Mycroft“, sagt John, und langsam hört der Hund auf.

„Hallo, Mr. Milverton“, sagt John. „Mein Name ist John; Sie kennen mich aus dem Sherlock-Holmes-Fanclub. Das ist meine Freundin Mary.“

„Hallo, John. Wie kann ich euch helfen?“

„Wir haben dieses Buch auf einem Flohmarkt gefunden.“ John zeigt ihm das Buch. „Und darin haben wir das entdeckt.“ Er gibt ihm das Stück Papier mit der Geheimschrift.

Mr. Milverton sieht sehr interessiert aus. „Das ist der Code der tanzenden Männchen! Habt ihr eine Übersetzung?“

„Ja. Es ist ein Brief von Conan Doyle.“ John gibt ihm die erste Seite der Übersetzung, aber nicht die zweite Seite mit den anderen Hinweisen.

Mr. Milverton liest sie. „Hm. Ich weiß nicht. Ich glaube, das ist eine Fälschung."

John ist enttäuscht. „Sind Sie sicher?"

„Ja, aber ihr könnt den Brief hierlassen. Ich habe eine Menge Bücher über Conan Doyle und kann sehen, ob ich etwas darüber herausfinden kann."

Mary findet, dass Mr. Milverton sehr begierig scheint, den Brief zu behalten. „Nein, danke", sagt sie. „Wir wollen ihn zurück."

Mr. Milverton sieht widerwillig aus, aber Mary hält ihm die Hand hin, und er gibt ihr den Brief.

„Danke", sagen Mary und John und verlassen den Laden.

05 | AT THE ROYAL OBSERVATORY

Demonstrative pronouns this/that/these/those

"That was strange," Mary says when they are outside the shop. "I don't **trust** Mr Milverton. And I don't think that this letter is fake."

"I think you're right," John says. "Do you think he wants the manuscript for himself?"

"**Perhaps**. We've got to be careful with this man."

John looks at his watch. "It's too late to go to Greenwich today. Let's meet tomorrow at half past 8."

The next day, they take the tube to Greenwich and walk through Greenwich Park to the Royal Observatory. **Unfortunately**, they cannot take Mycroft with them into the museum.

"He can wait outside," John says. "Let's **tie** him to this **bench** here."

They buy tickets and go in. "Look at those **signs** over there," Mary says. "There is one to the Octagon Room!"

"This must be it! Let's go there."

The Octagon Room is large with high windows, **wooden** walls and many clocks.

John takes out the secret letter and reads: "*In the Octagon, you find the numbers that lead you to the next clue.* – Okay, let's look for numbers."

Luckily, it is so early that no other people are in the room. The children look **closely** at the clocks. There are a lot of numbers on the clocks, but they have no idea which of these numbers are important.

After about 15 minutes, they are close to **giving up**. Mary sits down on the floor, frustrated.

Suddenly, her eyes widen. "Look, over there!" She **points** to the bottom of the wooden wall. "Those numbers!"

They hurry to the wall. At the bottom, and **barely visible**, are small numbers **scratched** into the dark wood:

51° 29' 57.8040" N
0° 7' 38.8740" W

Mary takes out a notebook and writes down the numbers. Then she looks at John: "What does it mean?"

What do you think? What do these strange numbers mean? The answer is in the next chapter.

Vocabulary

Englisch	Deutsch
to trust	vertrauen
perhaps	vielleicht
unfortunately	unglücklicherweise
to tie	binden, anbinden

the bench	die Parkbank, Sitzbank
the sign	das (Hinweis)Schild
wooden	hölzern
luckily	glücklicherweise
closely	genau
to give up	aufgeben
to point	zeigen
barely	kaum
visible	sichtbar
scratched	Vergangenheit von to scratch: ritzen

Gap text 1: Demonstrative pronouns

Fill in demonstrative pronouns *(this/that/these/those)*

"(1) ______ was strange," Mary says when they are outside the shop. "I don't **trust** Mr Milverton. And I don't think that (2) ______ letter is fake."

"I think you're right," John says. "Do you think he wants the manuscript for himself?"

"**Perhaps**. We've got to be careful with this man."

John looks at his watch. "It's too late to go to Greenwich today. Let's meet tomorrow at half past 8."

The next day, they take the tube to Greenwich and walk through Greenwich Park to the Royal Observatory. **Unfortunately**, they cannot take Mycroft with them into the museum.

"He can wait outside," John says. "Let's **tie** him to (3) ______ **bench** here."

They buy tickets and go in. "Look at (4) ______ **signs** over there," Mary says. "There is one to the Octagon Room!"

"This must be it! Let's go there."

The Octagon Room is large with high windows, **wooden** walls and many clocks.

John takes out the secret letter and reads: "*In the Octagon, you find the numbers that lead you to the next clue.* – Okay, let's look for numbers."

Luckily, it is so early that no other people are in the room. The children look **closely** at the clocks. There are a lot of numbers on the clocks, but they have no idea which of (5) ______ numbers are important.

After about 15 minutes, they are close to **giving up**. Mary sits down on the floor, frustrated.

Suddenly, her eyes widen. "Look, over there!" She points to the bottom of the wooden wall. "(6) ______ numbers!"

They hurry to the wall. At the bottom, and **barely visible**, are small numbers **scratched** into the dark wood:

51° 29' 57.8040" N
0° 7' 38.8740" W

Mary takes out a notebook and writes down the numbers. Then she looks at John: "What does it mean?"

Complete the sentences using *this, that, these, those*

(1) Look at ______ book here.
(2) John, is ______ your schoolbag over there?
(3) ____ are my parents and ______ people over there are my grandparents.
(4) Are ______ your exercise books here?
(5) ____ was a great film.
(6) ____ flowers over there are more beautiful than ______ flowers right here.

Find the words

strange – fake – manuscript – tomorrow – museum – clock – numbers – wood – notebook

M	S	T	A	B	O	V	W	Q	F
U	A	S	T	R	A	N	G	E	A
S	L	N	O	T	E	B	O	O	K
E	M	N	U	M	B	E	R	S	E
U	S	N	W	S	B	V	C	L	O
M	R	P	W	C	C	K	W	I	K
I	T	O	M	O	R	R	O	W	S
G	E	H	N	Z	O	L	I	E	R
J	S	V	W	H	E	D	S	P	C
H	L	C	L	O	C	K	E	I	T

Translation
IM KÖNIGLICHEN OBSERVATORIUM

„Das war seltsam“, sagt Mary, als sie vor dem Laden stehen. „Ich traue Mr. Milverton nicht. Und ich glaube nicht, dass dieser Brief gefälscht ist.“

„Ich glaube, du hast recht“, sagt John. „Glaubst du, er will das Manuskript für sich selbst?“

„Vielleicht. Wir müssen bei diesem Mann vorsichtig sein.“

John sieht auf seine Uhr. „Es ist zu spät, um heute noch nach Greenwich zu fahren. Treffen wir uns morgen um halb neun.“

Am nächsten Tag nehmen sie die U-Bahn nach Greenwich und gehen durch den Greenwich Park zum Königlichen Observatorium. Leider können sie Mycroft nicht mit in das Museum nehmen.

„Er kann draußen warten“, sagt John. „Binden wir ihn an diese Bank. „

Sie kaufen Eintrittskarten und gehen hinein. „Sieh dir die Schilder da drüben an“, sagt Mary. „Da ist eins zum Oktagon-Zimmer!“

„Das muss es sein! Lass uns hingehen.“

Das Oktagon-Zimmer ist groß, mit hohen Fenstern, Holzwänden und vielen Uhren.

John nimmt den geheimen Brief heraus und liest: *„Im Oktagon finden Sie die Zahlen, die Sie zum zweiten Ort führen.* - Okay, lasst uns nach Zahlen suchen.“

Zum Glück ist es noch so früh, dass sich keine anderen Leute im Raum befinden. Die Kinder sehen sich die Uhren genau an. Es sind viele Zahlen auf den Uhren, aber sie haben keine Ahnung, welche dieser Zahlen wichtig sind.

Nach etwa 15 Minuten sind sie kurz davor, aufzugeben. Mary setzt sich frustriert auf den Boden.

Plötzlich weiten sich ihre Augen. „Seht mal, da drüben!“ Sie zeigt auf den untersten Teil der Holzwand. „Diese Zahlen!“

Sie eilen zu der Wand. Am unteren Ende, kaum sichtbar, sind

kleine Zahlen in das dunkle Holz geritzt:

51° 29' 57.8040" N
0° 7' 38.8740" W

Mary nimmt ein Notizbuch heraus und schreibt die Zahlen auf. Dann sieht sie John an: „Was bedeutet das?“

06 | MYCROFT'S ADVENTURE

Can and must

John's dog, Mycroft, must wait outside the Observatory. He is **bored**. Because he is **tied** to the **bench**, he cannot do anything interesting.

"Why mustn't I go inside?" he thinks. "I want to help John, not stay outside."

Suddenly, Mycroft sees a squirrel on a tree not far away. "Squirrel!" He stands up. "I must **catch** it! I must get free from this bench!"

He pulls at the **lead** and is free after a few seconds. Mycroft runs towards the squirrel and **barks**, but he can't climb the tree. After a few minutes, the squirrel jumps to another tree and then to another. "I must **follow** it!" Mycroft thinks. He runs after the squirrel for a long time but cannot catch it.

Finally, he can't see the squirrel **anymore**. Mycroft knows that now he must return to John. He looks around. "Oh no," he thinks, "I'm **lost**! I have got no idea where I am!"

Mycroft runs around, trying to return to the Observatory, but he cannot find it. Finally, he lies down and **howls miserably**.

After a few minutes, another dog **crouches** next to him. It is a black and white border collie. "Hi," he says, "I'm Sherlock. What's the matter?"

"I **ran** after a squirrel and cannot find my way back to my master." Mycroft howls again.

"I can help you," the other dog says. "I know this park very well."

Mycroft feels much better. "I must get back to a large building," he says.

"There is only one large building in this park. I can take you there. But I mustn't lose my own master. Wait here." And Sherlock runs away.

After a few minutes, Sherlock comes back with a boy. "This is my master, Luke."

Luke pets Mycroft. "Hi you, did you run away?" Sherlock barks, and Mycroft howls.

Sherlock then tells Mycroft, "Come!" and runs towards the Observatory. Mycroft and Luke follow.

It is not far to the Observatory. "That's the building!" Mycroft barks at Sherlock.

John and Mary are standing at the bench, looking worried. "Mycroft!" John shouts when he sees him. "Why are you always running away?! You really must stop that!"

"Is this your dog?" Luke asks.

"Yes, thank you so much."

"You're welcome."

"Thank you," Mycroft barks at Sherlock.

"No problem," Sherlock barks back, "but stay with your master now. **That was a close one**."

Vocabulary

Englisch	Deutsch
the adventure	das Abenteuer
to be bored	gelangweilt sein
to be tied	angebunden sein
to catch	fangen
the lead	die Leine
to bark	bellen
to follow	folgen
not anymore	nicht mehr
to be lost	sich verirren
to howl	heulen
miserably	unglücklich
to crouch	sich hinkauern
ran	Vergangenheit von to run: rennen
That was a close one.	Das war knapp.

Gap text 1: Can and must

Fill in *can/cannot/can't or must/must not/mustn't*

John's dog, Mycroft, (1) ______ wait outside the Observatory. He is **bored**. Because he is **tied** to the bench, he (2) ______ do anything interesting.

"Why (3) ______ I go inside?" he thinks. "I want to help John, not stay outside."

Suddenly, Mycroft sees a squirrel on a tree not far away. "Squirrel!" He stands up. "I must **catch** it! I (4) ______ get free from this bench!"

He pulls at the **lead** and is free after a few seconds. Mycroft runs towards the squirrel and **barks**, but he (5) ______ climb the tree. After a few minutes, the squirrel jumps to another tree and then to another. "I (6) ______ **follow** it!" Mycroft thinks. He runs after the squirrel for a long time but (7) ______ catch it.

Finally, he can't see the squirrel **anymore**. Mycroft knows that now he (8) ______ return to John. He looks around. "Oh no," he thinks, "I'm **lost**! I have got no idea where I am!"

Mycroft runs around, trying to return to the Observatory, but he (9) ______ find it. Finally, he lies down and **howls miserably**.

After a few minutes, another dog **crouches** next to him. It is a black and white border collie. "Hi," he says, "I'm Sherlock. What's the matter?"

"I **ran** after a squirrel and cannot find my way back to my master." Mycroft howls again.

"I (10) ______ help you," the other dog says. "I know this park very well."

Mycroft feels much better. "I must get back to a large building," he says.

"There is only one large building in this park. I (11) ______ take you there. But I (12) ______ lose my own master. Wait here." And Sherlock runs away.

After a few minutes, Sherlock comes back with a boy. "This is my master, Luke."

Luke pets Mycroft. "Hi you, did you run away?" Sherlock barks, and Mycroft howls.

Sherlock then tells Mycroft, "Come!" and runs towards the Observatory. Mycroft and Luke follow.

It is not far to the Observatory. "That's the building!" Mycroft barks at Sherlock.

John and Mary are standing at the bench, looking worried.

"Mycroft!" John shouts when he sees him. "Why are you always running away?! You really (13) ______ stop that!"

"Is this your dog?" Luke asks.

"Yes, thank you so much."

"You're welcome."

"Thank you," Mycroft barks at Sherlock.

"No problem," Sherlock barks back, "but stay with your master now. **That was a close one**."

Answer the questions about the story

(1) Why is Mycroft bored?
(2) Why does Mycroft run away?
(3) Who finds Mycroft and helps him?
(4) What kind of dog is Sherlock?

(1) ____

(2) ____

(3) ____

(4) ____

Build questions with *can* and *must*

Example:
She can play the piano. => *Can she play the piano?*

(1) We must go shopping today.
(2) I can see my friend.

(3) You can ride a bike.
(4) She must do her homework.
(5) They can dance.

(1) ______________________________

(2) ______________________________

(3) ______________________________

(4) ______________________________

(5) ______________________________

Translation
MYCROFTS ABENTEUER

Mycroft, der Hund von John, muss vor dem Observatorium warten. Er langweilt sich. Weil er an die Bank gebunden ist, kann er nichts Interessantes tun.

„Warum darf ich nicht hineingehen?" denkt er. „Ich will John helfen und nicht draußen bleiben."

Plötzlich sieht Mycroft nicht weit entfernt ein Eichhörnchen auf einem Baum. „Eichhörnchen!" Er steht auf. „Ich muss es fangen! Ich muss mich von dieser Bank befreien!"

Er zieht an der Leine und ist nach ein paar Sekunden frei. Mycroft rennt auf das Eichhörnchen zu und bellt, aber es kann nicht auf den Baum klettern. Nach ein paar Minuten springt das Eichhörnchen zu einem anderen Baum und dann zu einem anderen. „Ich muss ihm folgen!" denkt Mycroft. Er rennt dem Eichhörnchen lange hinterher, kann es aber nicht einholen.

Schließlich kann er das Eichhörnchen nicht mehr sehen. Mycroft weiß, dass er jetzt zu John zurückkehren muss. Er sieht sich um.

„Oh nein“, denkt er, „ich habe mich verirrt! Ich habe keine Ahnung, wo ich bin!“

Mycroft rennt herum und versucht, zum Observatorium zurückzukehren, aber er kann es nicht finden. Schließlich legt er sich hin und heult jämmerlich.

Nach ein paar Minuten kauert sich ein anderer Hund neben ihn. Es ist ein schwarz-weißer Border Collie. „Hallo“, sagt er, „ich bin Sherlock. Was ist mit dir los?“

„Ich bin einem Eichhörnchen hinterhergerannt und kann nicht zu meinem Herrchen zurückfinden.“ Mycroft heult wieder.

„Ich kann dir helfen“, sagt der andere Hund. „Ich kenne diesen Park sehr gut.“

Mycroft fühlt sich viel besser. „Ich muss zurück zu einem großen Gebäude“, sagt er.

„In diesem Park gibt es nur ein einziges großes Gebäude. Ich kann dich dorthin bringen. Aber ich darf meinen eigenen Herrn nicht verlieren. Warte hier.“ Und Sherlock rennt weg.

Nach ein paar Minuten kommt Sherlock mit einem Jungen zurück. „Das ist mein Herrchen, Luke.“

Luke streichelt Mycroft. „Hallo du, bist du weggelaufen?“ Sherlock bellt, und Mycroft heult auf.

Dann sagt Sherlock zu Mycroft: „Komm!“, und rennt zum Observatorium. Mycroft und Luke folgen ihm.

Es ist nicht weit bis zum Observatorium. „Das ist das Gebäude!“ bellt Mycroft Sherlock zu.

John und Mary stehen bei der Bank und sehen besorgt aus. „Mycroft!“ ruft John, als er ihn sieht. „Warum läufst du immer weg?! Du musst wirklich damit aufhören!“

„Ist das dein Hund?“ fragt Luke.

„Ja, vielen Dank.“

„Gern geschehen.“

„Danke“, bellt Mycroft Sherlock an.

„Kein Problem“, bellt Sherlock zurück, „aber bleib jetzt bei deinem Herrchen. Das war ganz schön knapp.“

07 | IN WESTMINSTER ABBEY

Do and does

Luke and Sherlock walk away, and Mary and John sit down on the bench outside the Royal Observatory. Mary takes out her notebook, and they look at the strange numbers from the Octagon Room.

"Do you know what that means?" John asks.

Mary shakes her head. "I have no idea."

They look at the numbers for several minutes. Suddenly, Mary says, "Wait, I know this from school."

"Really?"

"Yes, from geography. These are **coordinates**."

"Oh yes," John says, "I remember. So these numbers are a place?"

"Yes, I think so. Does your mobile phone have an app to **enter** coordinates?"

"I don't know. Let's try it out."

John searches through the apps on his mobile. "I think this is right." He enters the numbers. "Look, this is **Westminster Abbey**, isn't it?"

"Yes. So, do we have to go there?"

"I think we do," John replies. "But what does it say in the letter? *'Mr Scrooge will help you'*. Does Charles Dickens have anything to do with Westminster Abbey?"

"I don't know. Let's go there and find out."

They take the tube to Westminster Abbey and walk into the church. It is very large, and they do not know where to start.

"Excuse me," John asks a **guard**. "Does Charles Dickens have anything to do with Westminster Abbey?"

"Yes," the guard says, "he's **buried** here. There is a whole area with writers in the church."

"Great! Where is his **grave**?"

The guard shows them the way. When the children **arrive** at the grave, they read:

Charles Dickens
Born 7th February 1812
Died 9th June 1870

"What does the clue from the letter say?" Mary asks.

John takes out the piece of paper:

1=15, 2=4, 3=9, 4=20, 5=35, 6=7, 7=2, 8=M, 9=26, 10=14, 11=6, 12=42, 13=M 14=17, 15=16, 16=7, 17=12, 18=39, 19=39, 20=3.

"Doesn't this look like another code?" Mary asks.

"I think you are right," John says. "Perhaps the **inscription** on the grave gives us the letters for the next location."

"Let's write it down," Mary says, taking out her notebook.

They **leave** the church and sit down on a bench. Mary **numbers** each letter from the inscription on the grave. "So, the first letter we need is letter 15 from the inscription. That's a 'B'. Then the second letter is letter 4 from the inscription, that's an 'R'".

They go on until they are finished. Then they smile at each other. "Let's go to the…."

Can you solve the code? Where do they have to go next? The answer is in the next chapter.

Vocabulary

Englisch	Deutsch
the coordinates	die geographischen Koordinaten
to enter	eingeben
Westminster Abbey	Westminster Abbey ist eine große Kirche in London.
the guard	der Wächter
buried	Vergangenheit von to bury: begraben/graben
the grave	das Grab
to arrive	ankommen
the inscription	die Inschrift
to leave	verlassen
to number	nummerieren

Gap text 1: Do and does

Fill in *do/does, do not/does not or don't/doesn't*

Luke and Sherlock walk away, and Mary and John sit down on the bench outside the Royal Observatory. Mary takes out her notebook, and they look at the strange numbers from the Octagon Room.

"(1) ______ you know what that means?" John asks.

Mary shakes her head. "I have no idea."

They look at the numbers for several minutes. Suddenly, Mary says, "Wait, I know this from school."

"Really?"

"Yes, from geography. These are **coordinates**."

"Oh yes," John says, "I remember. So these numbers are a place?"

"Yes, I think so. (2) ______ your mobile phone have an app to **enter** coordinates?"

"I (3) ______ know. Let's try it out."

John searches through the apps on his mobile. "I think this is right." He enters the numbers. "Look, this is **Westminster Abbey**, isn't it?"

"Yes. So, do we have to go there?"

"I think we (4) ____," John replies. "But what (5) ______ it say in the letter? *'Mr Scrooge will help you'*. (6) ______ Charles Dickens have anything to do with Westminster Abbey?"

"I (7) ______ know. Let's go there and find out."

They take the tube to Westminster Abbey and walk into the church. It is very large, and they (8) ______ know where to start.

"Excuse me," John asks a **guard**. "Does Charles Dickens have anything to do with Westminster Abbey?"

"Yes," the guard says, "he's **buried** here. There is a whole area with writers in the church."

"Great! Where is his **grave**?"

The guard shows them the way. When the children **arrive** at the grave, they read:

Charles Dickens
Born 7th February 1812
Died 9th June 1870

"What (9) ______ the clue from the letter say?" Mary asks.

John takes out the piece of paper:

1=15, 2=4, 3=9, 4=20, 5=35, 6=7, 7=2, 8=M, 9=26, 10=14, 11=6, 12=42, 13=M 14=17, 15=16, 16=7, 17=12, 18=39, 19=39, 20=3.

"(10) ______ this look like another code?" Mary asks.

"I think you are right," John says. "Perhaps the **inscription** on the grave gives us the letters for the next location."

"Let's write it down," Mary says, taking out her notebook.

They **leave** the church and sit down on a bench. Mary **numbers** each letter from the inscription on the grave. "So, the first letter we need is letter 15 from the inscription. That's a 'B'. Then the second letter is letter 4 from the inscription, that's an 'R'".

They go on until they are finished. Then they smile at each other. "Let's go to the…."

Bring the words into the correct order

1)	means?	you know	Do	that	what
2)	from school	I	this	know	
3)	searches through	John	his mobile	on	the apps
4)	takes out	of paper	John	piece	the
5)	finished	They	until	go on	they are

Answer the questions about the story

(1) Does John know what the numbers mean?
(2) Does John's mobile phone have an app to enter coordinates?
(3) Do Mary and John have to go to Westminster Abbey?
(4) Does Charles Dickens have anything to do with Westminster Abbey?
(5) Do the children understand the code from the grave?

(1) ____

(2) ____

(3) ____

(4) ____

(5) ____

Translation

IN WESTMINSTER ABBEY

Luke und Sherlock gehen weg, und Mary und John setzen sich auf die Bank vor dem Königlichen Observatorium. Mary holt ihr Notizbuch heraus, und sie sehen sich die seltsamen Zahlen aus dem Oktagon-Zimmer an.

„Weißt du, was das bedeutet?" fragt John.

Mary schüttelt den Kopf. „Ich habe keine Ahnung."

Sie betrachten die Zahlen mehrere Minuten lang. Plötzlich sagt Mary: „Warte, das kenne ich aus der Schule."

„Wirklich?"

„Ja, aus Geographie. Das sind Koordinaten."

„Oh ja", sagt John, „ich erinnere mich. Diese Zahlen sind also ein Ort?"

„Ja, ich glaube schon. Hat dein Handy eine App, um Koordinaten einzugeben?"

„Ich weiß es nicht. Lass es uns ausprobieren."

John durchsucht die Apps auf seinem Handy. „Ich glaube, das ist richtig." Er gibt die Zahlen ein. „Sieh mal, das ist Westminster Abbey, nicht wahr?"

„Ja. Müssen wir dorthin gehen?"

„Ich glaube schon", antwortet John. „Aber was steht in dem Brief? *'Mr. Scrooge wird dir helfen'*. Hat Charles Dickens etwas mit Westminster Abbey zu tun?"

„Ich weiß es nicht. Lass uns hinfahren und es herausfinden."

Sie nehmen die U-Bahn nach Westminster Abbey und gehen in die Kirche. Sie ist sehr groß, und sie wissen nicht, wo sie anfangen sollen.

„Entschuldigen Sie", fragt John einen Wachmann. „Hat Charles Dickens etwas mit Westminster Abbey zu tun?"

„Ja", sagt der Wächter, „er ist hier begraben. In der Kirche gibt es einen ganzen Bereich mit Schriftstellern."

„Toll! Wo ist sein Grab?"

Der Wächter zeigt ihnen den Weg. Als die Kinder beim Grab ankommen, lesen sie:

Charles Dickens
Geboren am 7. Februar 1812
Gestorben am 9. Juni 1870

„Was steht auf dem Hinweis im Brief?" fragt Mary.

John nimmt den Zettel heraus:

1=15, 2=4, 3=9, 4=20, 5=35, 6=7, 7=2, 8=M, 9=26, 10=14, 11=6, 12=42, 13=M 14=17, 15=16, 16=7, 17=12, 18=39, 19=39, 20=3.

„Sieht das nicht wie ein weiterer Code aus?" fragt Mary.

„Ich glaube, du hast recht", sagt John. „Vielleicht gibt uns die Inschrift auf dem Grab die Buchstaben für den nächsten Ort."

„Schreiben wir die Inschrift auf", sagt Mary und nimmt ihr Notizbuch heraus.

Sie verlassen die Kirche und setzen sich auf eine Bank. Mary nummeriert jeden Buchstaben der Grabinschrift. „Also, der erste Buchstabe, den wir brauchen, ist Buchstabe 15 der Inschrift. Das ist ein 'B'. Der zweite Buchstabe ist der 4. aus der Inschrift, das ist ein 'R'". Sie machen weiter, bis sie fertig sind. Dann lächeln sie sich gegenseitig an. „Lass uns ins .... gehen".

08 | TAKING THE BUS

Question words: where, who, what, how, why, when

"…let's go to the **British Museum**!"

"But the code says 'British Museum Rosetta'," Mary says. "What is 'Rosetta'?"

"That must be the Rosetta Stone," John explains. "I know that it is in the British Museum. It's a big black stone used to decipher **hieroglyphs**."

"How?" asks Mary.

"On the Stone is the same text in three languages and **scripts**. So when you **compare** all three, you can see which hieroglyphic signs stand for which letters and what they mean."

"Do you know who **found out** about this?" Mary asks.

"I think it **was** a Frenchman called **Champollion**," John says.

"When was that?"

"About 200 years ago."

"Why do you know this?"

John smiles. "Because I like codes. Do you want to go to the museum?"

"Of course. How far is it from here? Can we walk?"

John looks at his mobile. “We can, but it takes about 40 minutes.”

“Uff, that’s long,” Mary says. “How else can we get there?”

“Let me check. I think we can take the bus. We have to **change** once, but it’s faster than walking.”

“Okay, where do we have to go?”

John looks at his phone again. “Over there is the bus stop. We need bus number 24.”

They walk to the bus stop and wait for a few minutes until the bus **arrives**. It’s a double-decker bus, and they go up to the upper level and sit right at the front. There’s a lot of **traffic**, and the bus has to stop and wait several times. Mycroft is nervous and **growls**.

“What is the matter with him?” Mary asks.

“I don’t know. Usually, he likes buses,” John says.

After 18 minutes, they get off the bus.

“Where do we have to go now?” Mary asks.

“We can stay at this bus stop and wait for bus number 14.”

The bus arrives soon, but when they sit down, Mycroft starts to growl again.

“What is the matter with you?” John asks him, trying to **calm** him **down**. But Mycroft doesn’t stop growling. He looks at a man with a big **beard** and sunglasses who sits a few seats away.

“I think we should get off the bus,” Mary says.

“Yes, let’s do that. We’re not far from the museum.” They get off at the next stop.

John looks at his phone again. “Oh no, my **battery is low**! I think my phone will be dead soon.”

“But how will we be able to find our way around?”

“Don’t worry,” John says, “we can always **ask** people **for directions**, and there are maps of the tube in the stations.”

Vocabulary

Englisch	Deutsch
British Museum	Eines der größten und wichtigsten Museen der Welt
the hieroglyphs	die Hieroglyphen (Schrift der alten Ägypter)
the script	die Schrift, Schriftart
to compare	vergleichen
found out	Vergangenheit von to find out: herausfinden
was	Vergangenheit von to be (is): ist
Champollion	Jean-François Champollion (1790-1832), Entzifferer der Hieroglyphen.
to change	umsteigen
to arrive	ankommen
the traffic	der Verkehr
to growl	knurren
to calm down	jemanden/sich beruhigen
the beard	der Bart
The battery is low.	Der Akku ist fast leer.
to ask for directions	nach dem Weg fragen

Gap text 1: Question words

Fill in question words *(where, who, what, how, why, when)*

"…let's go to the **British Museum**!"

"But the code says 'British Museum Rosetta'," Mary says. "(1) ______ is 'Rosetta'?"

"That must be the Rosetta Stone," John explains. "I know that it is in the British Museum. It's a big black stone used to decipher **hieroglyphs**."

"(2) ____?" asks Mary.

"On the Stone is the same text in three languages and **scripts**. So when you **compare** all three, you can see which hieroglyphic signs stand for which letters and (3) ______ they mean."

"Do you know (4) ______ **found out** about this?" Mary asks.

"I think it was a Frenchman called **Champollion**," John says. "

"(5) ______ was that?"

"About 200 years ago."

"(6) ______ do you know this?"

John smiles. "Because I like codes. Do you want to go to the museum?"

"Of course. (7) ______ far is it from here? Can we walk?"

John looks at his mobile. "We can, but it takes about 40 minutes."

"Uff, that's long," Mary says. "How else can we get there?"

"Let me check. I think we can take the bus. We have to **change** once, but it's faster than walking."

"Okay, (8) _____ do we have to go?"

John looks at his phone again. "Over there is the bus stop. We need bus number 24."

They walk to the bus stop and wait for a few minutes until the bus **arrives**. It's a double-decker bus, and they go up to the upper level and sit right at the front. There's a lot of **traffic**, and the bus has to stop and wait several times. Mycroft is nervous and **growls**.

"What is the matter with him?" Mary asks.

"I don't know. Usually, he likes buses," John says.

After 18 minutes, they get off the bus.

"(9) ______ do we have to go now?" Mary asks.

"We can stay at this bus stop and wait for bus number 14."

The bus arrives soon, but when they sit down, Mycroft starts to growl again.

"(10) ______ is the matter with you?" John asks him, trying to **calm** him **down**. But Mycroft doesn't stop growling. He looks at a man with a big **beard** and sunglasses who sits a few seats away.

"I think we should get off the bus," Mary says.

"Yes, let's do that. We're not far from the museum." They get off at the next stop.

John looks at his phone again. "Oh no, **my battery is low**! I think my phone will be dead soon."

"But (11) ______ will we be able to find our way around?"

"Don't worry," John says, "we can always **ask** people **for directions**, and there are maps of the tube in the stations."

Form questions with question words

Example:

John and Mary take the bus. => What do John and Mary take?

(1) The Rosetta Stone is in the British Museum.
(2) The Rosetta Stone is a big black stone used to decipher hieroglyphs.
(3) Jean-François Champollion deciphered the hieroglyphs.
(4) It takes about 40 minutes to walk to the museum.
(5) John knows about Jean François Champollion because he likes codes.
(6) Jean-François Champollion deciphered the hieroglyphs about 200 years ago.

(1) ____________________

(2) ____________________

(3) ____________________

(4) ____________________

(5) ____________________

(6) ____________________

Match the words with the correct translation

(1) language	a) Karte, Landkarte
(2) bus stop	b) Sonnenbrille
(3) soon	c) fragen
(4) sunglasses	d) bald
(5) to ask	e) Sprache
(6) map	f) Bushaltestelle

Translation

DIE BUSFAHRT

„...lass uns ins Britische Museum gehen!"

„Aber der Code ergibt 'British Museum Rosetta'", sagt Mary. „Was ist 'Rosetta'?"

„Das muss der Stein von Rosetta sein", erklärt John. „Ich weiß, dass er im Britischen Museum ist. Es ist ein großer schwarzer Stein, mit dem man Hieroglyphen entziffern kann."

„Wie?", fragt Mary.

„Auf dem Stein steht derselbe Text in drei Sprachen und Schriften. Wenn man also alle drei vergleicht, kann man sehen, welche Hieroglyphenzeichen für welche Buchstaben stehen und was sie bedeuten."

„Weißt du, wer das herausgefunden hat?" fragt Mary.

„Ich glaube es war ein Franzose namens Champollion", sagt John.

„Wann war das?"

„Vor ungefähr 200 Jahren."

„Warum weißt du das?"

John lächelt. „Weil ich Codes mag. Willst du ins Museum gehen?“

„Ja, natürlich. Wie weit ist es von hier? Können wir laufen?“

John sieht auf sein Handy. „Das können wir, aber es dauert ungefähr 40 Minuten.“

„Uff, das ist lang“, sagt Mary. „Wie können wir sonst dorthin kommen?“

„Lass mich nachsehen. Ich glaube, wir können den Bus nehmen. Wir müssen zwar einmal umsteigen, aber es ist schneller als zu Fuß.“

„Okay, wo müssen wir denn hin?“

John sieht wieder auf sein Handy. „Da drüben ist die Bushaltestelle. Wir brauchen die Buslinie 24.“

Sie gehen zur Bushaltestelle und warten ein paar Minuten, bis der Bus eintrifft. Es ist ein Doppeldeckerbus, und sie gehen in die obere Etage und setzen sich ganz nach vorne. Es ist viel Verkehr, und der Bus muss mehrmals anhalten und warten. Mycroft ist nervös und knurrt.

„Was ist denn mit ihm los?“ fragt Mary.

„Ich weiß es nicht. Normalerweise mag er Busse“, sagt John.

Nach 18 Minuten steigen sie aus dem Bus aus.

„Wohin müssen wir jetzt gehen?“ fragt Mary.

„Wir können an dieser Haltestelle bleiben und auf den Bus Nummer 14 warten.“

Der Bus kommt bald, aber als sie sich hinsetzen, fängt Mycroft wieder an zu knurren.

„Was ist denn los mit dir?“ fragt John ihn und versucht, ihn zu beruhigen. Aber Mycroft hört nicht auf zu knurren. Er blickt zu einem Mann mit einem dicken Bart und einer Sonnenbrille, der ein paar Plätze weiter sitzt.

„Ich denke, wir sollten aussteigen“, sagt Mary.

„Ja, das sollten wir tun. Wir sind nicht weit vom Museum entfernt.“ Sie steigen an der nächsten Haltestelle aus.

John sieht wieder auf sein Handy. „Oh nein, mein Akku ist fast leer! Ich glaube, mein Handy wird bald tot sein.“

„Aber wie sollen wir uns dann zurechtfinden?“

„Keine Sorge", sagt John, „wir können immer Leute nach dem Weg fragen, und in den U-Bahn-Stationen gibt es U-Bahn-Pläne."

09 | AT THE BRITISH MUSEUM

Present simple

A few minutes later, they see the British Museum, a grand building with **columns** in front. It looks very **impressive**.

Mary and John walk into the museum and look around. They are in a big, **bright entrance hall** with a **cupula**. There are lots of people.

"Let's ask one of the guards," Mary says and walks towards a woman in a guard uniform. "Excuse me, I have a question. Where can we find the Rosetta Stone?"

The guard smiles at them. "Are you interested in **Ancient Egypt**?"

"Yes, very much," John says.

"It's right over there," the guard **points** to the left. "Go through the door there, and then you can see it."

They **follow her instructions** and soon see the black stone.

"What does the clue from the letter say?" Mary asks.

John takes out the piece of paper. "It says '***folded cloth*** – ***quail***

chick – *quail chick*'. Can you see anything like that here?"

They look around but don't find anything.

Suddenly, they see the nice guard walking towards them. "The stone is very interesting, isn't it?" She says to the children.

"Yes," Mary replies.

"Do you want to learn how to write in hieroglyphs?"

The children **nod**.

"Look, over there, you can see the alphabet in hieroglyphs." The guard points to a large **table**, which hangs a few metres away on the wall.

"Thank you very much," John says. "We will take a look."

The guard smiles again. "You're welcome," she says before turning back towards the entrance hall.

Mary and John go over to the table and look closely at the hieroglyphs.

"Look!" John whispers excitedly to Mary, "There's a hieroglyphic sign called 'quail chick'."

"Yes, and there is one called 'folded cloth'", Mary says.

"So what does it mean?" Mary asks. "'Folded cloth' stands for the letter 'S', and 'quail chick' for 'O', 'U' or 'W'. So if the code is '*folded cloth – quail chick – quail chick*', the word we are looking for is either '*SOO*', '*SUU*' or '*SWW*'"?

John shakes his head. "I really don't know."

Can you help Mary and John? What is their next location? The answer is in the next chapter.

Vocabulary

Englisch	Deutsch
the column	die Säule
impressive	beeindruckend
bright	hell
the entrance hall	die Eingangshalle
the cupola	die Kuppel
Ancient Egypt	das Alte Ägypten
to point	zeigen
to follow instructions	Anweisungen befolgen
folded	Vergangenheit von to fold: falten
the cloth	der Stoff, das Tuch
the quail chick	das Wachtelküken
to nod	nicken
the table	die Tafel

Gap text 1: Present simple

Fill in verbs in the present simple

A few minutes later, they (1) ______ (see) the British Museum, a grand building with **columns** in front. It (2) ______ (look) very **impressive**.

Mary and John walk into the museum and look around. They are in a big, **bright entrance hall** with a **cupula**. There are lots of people.

"Let's ask one of the guards," Mary (3) ______ (say) and walks towards a woman in a guard uniform. "Excuse me, I have a question. Where can we find the Rosetta Stone?"

The guard (4) ______ (smile) at them. "Are you interested in **Ancient Egypt**?"

"Yes, very much," John says.

"It's right over there," the guard **points** to the left. "Go through the door there, and then you can see it."

They **follow her instructions** and soon (5) ______ (see) the black stone.

"What (6) ______ (do) the clue from the letter say?" Mary asks.

John takes out the piece of paper. "It says '***folded cloth*** – ***quail chick*** – *quail chick*'. Can you see anything like that here?"

They (7) ______ (look) around but don't find anything.

Suddenly, they see the nice guard walking towards them. "The stone is very interesting, isn't it?" She says to the children.

"Yes," Mary replies.

"Do you want to learn how to write in hieroglyphs?"

The children **nod**.

"Look, over there, you can (8) ______ (see) the alphabet in hieroglyphs." The guard points to a large **table**, which hangs a few metres away on the wall.

"Thank you very much," John says. "We will take a look."

The guard smiles again. "You're welcome," she (9) ______ (say) before turning back towards the entrance hall.

Mary and John (10) ______ (go) over to the table and look closely at the hieroglyphs.

"Look!" John whispers excitedly to Mary, "There's a hieroglyphic sign called 'quail chick'."

"Yes, and there is one called 'folded cloth'", Mary says.

"So what (11) ______ (do) it mean?" Mary asks. "'Folded cloth' stands for the letter 'S', and 'quail chick' for 'O', 'U' or 'W'. So if the code is '*folded cloth – quail chick – quail chick*', the word we are looking for is either '*SOO*', '*SUU*' or '*SWW*'"?

John (12) ______ (shake) his head. "I really don't know."

Complete the sentences

"He, she, it, das *-s* muss mit" – but what is the correct form?

(1) Every day, Mary ______ (eats / eates) muesli in the morning.
(2) My father ______ (washs / washes) the dishes.
(3) ____ (Dos / Does) she like to go to school?
(4) He ______ (trys / tries) on a new pullover.
(5) My mother ______ (plays / plaies) the piano.
(6) John ______ (relaxs /relaxes) in the garden.
(7) "Hurry up!" ______ (says / sais) Mary.

Translation

IM BRITISCHEN MUSEUM

Ein paar Minuten später sehen sie das Britische Museum, ein großes Gebäude mit Säulen davor. Es sieht sehr beeindruckend aus.

Mary und John betreten das Museum und sehen sich um. Sie befinden sich in einer großen, hellen Eingangshalle mit einer Kuppel. Die Halle ist voller Leute.

„Fragen wir doch einen der Wächter", sagt Mary und geht auf eine Frau in einer Wächteruniform zu. „Entschuldigen Sie, ich habe eine Frage. Wo können wir den Stein von Rosetta finden?"

Die Wächterin lächelt sie an. „Interessiert ihr euch für das alte Ägypten?"

„Ja, sehr sogar", sagt John.

„Er ist gleich da drüben", die Wächterin zeigt nach links. „Geht durch die Tür dort, dann könnt ihr ihn sehen."

Sie folgen ihren Anweisungen und sehen bald den schwarzen Stein.

„Was sagt der Hinweis aus dem Brief?" fragt Mary.

John nimmt das Stück Papier heraus. „Da steht *‚gefaltetes Tuch - Wachtelküken – Wachtelküken*‘. Kannst du hier so etwas sehen?"

Sie sehen sich um, finden aber nichts.

Plötzlich sehen sie die nette Wächterin auf sie zukommen. „Der Stein ist sehr interessant, nicht wahr?" sagt sie zu den Kindern.

„Ja", antwortet Mary.

„Wollt ihr lernen, wie man mit Hieroglyphen schreibt?"

Die Kinder nicken.

„Schaut, dort drüben könnt ihr das Alphabet in Hieroglyphen sehen." Die Wächterin zeigt auf eine große Tafel, die ein paar Meter entfernt an der Wand hängt.

„Vielen Dank", sagt John. „Wir werden es uns ansehen."

Die Wächterin lächelt wieder. „Gern geschehen", sagt sie, bevor sie wieder zurück in die Eingangshalle geht.

Mary und John gehen zu der Tafel und sehen sich die Hieroglyphen genau an.

„Sieh mal!" flüstert John Mary aufgeregt zu: „Da ist ein Hieroglyphenzeichen das ‚Wachtelküken‘ heißt."

„Ja, und es gibt eines das ‚gefaltetes Tuch‘ heißt", sagt Mary.

„Und was bedeutet es dann?" fragt Mary. „‚Gefaltetes Tuch‘ steht für den Buchstaben ‚S‘, und ‚Wachtelküken‘ für ‚O‘, ‚U‘ oder ‚W‘. Wenn der Code also *‚gefaltetes Tuch - Wachtelküken – Wachtelküken*‘ lautet, ist das gesuchte Wort entweder *‚SOO*‘, *‚SUU*‘ oder *‚SWW*?"

John schüttelt den Kopf. „Ich weiß es wirklich nicht."

10 | THE STRANGE MAN

Present progressive and present simple

"'*SWW*' sounds **unlikely**," Mary says, "but what about '*SOO*' or '*SUU*'?"

An old woman who is standing next to them turns towards the children. "What are you talking about? This isn't the zoo. It's a museum!"

John and Mary laugh out loud. "Of course, the zoo! Thank you very much!"

The older woman **shakes** her head and walks away.

"So we have to get to the London Zoo," John says. "But how do we get there?"

"I **went** to the zoo with my parents last month," Mary says. "I think we can take the tube to Baker Street."

"Alright, but where is the next tube station?"

"I´m not sure. Let's ask the nice guard."

They return to the entrance hall, where the guard still stands, and ask her.

"The closest underground station is Tottenham Court Road," she says, telling them how to get there.

"Thank you," the children reply and leave the museum.

When they reach the tube station, they look for a tube map.

"Look," Mary says, pointing at the map. "We are here, and we can take the black line to Charing Cross and then the brown line to Baker Street."

Suddenly, Mycroft starts growling again.

"Sh, Mycroft, quiet! What's the matter with you?" While John is trying to calm Mycroft down, Mary looks around.

"Strange, that man with the beard and the sunglasses who was on the bus is standing over there and reading a newspaper! Mycroft really doesn't like him. Wait, isn't that the guy from the antique shop?"

John looks at him. "Mr Milverton from the Sherlock Holmes fan club? But why is he wearing a **disguise**?"

"I think he is following us to find the manuscript!"

John looks very angry. "I think you are right. Let's try to **mislead** him."

Mycroft is still growling, but John ignores him and looks at the map again. Very loudly, he says, "There, let's take the black line to Embankment and then the green line to Tower Hill. From there we can walk to the Tower. Let's go."

And they quickly walk down the stairs towards the underground trains.

When the next train arrives, John and Mary step inside. They **notice** that the man with the beard also gets on the train a few doors further down. At the last moment, when the doors are closing, the children and Mycroft jump out of the train. The man with the beard looks shocked and angry, but the train is already moving.

They wait for the next train and step inside.

Vocabulary

Englisch	Deutsch
unlikely	unwahrscheinlich
to shake	schütteln
went	Vergangenheit von to go: gehen
the disguise	die Verkleidung
to mislead	in die Irre führen
to notice	bemerken, wahrnehmen

Gap text 1: Present progressive and present simple

Fill in verbs in the present progressive or present simple

"'*SWW*' sounds **unlikely**," Mary says, "but what about '*SOO*' or '*SUU*'?"

An old woman who is (1) ______ (stand) next to them turns towards the children. "What are you (2) ______ (talk) about? This isn't the zoo. It's a museum!"

John and Mary laugh out loud. "Of course, the zoo! Thank you very much!"

The older woman **shakes** her head and (3) ______ (walk) away.

"So we have to get to the London Zoo," John says. "But how do we get there?"

"I **went** to the zoo with my parents last month," Mary says. "I think we can take the tube to Baker Street."

"Alright, but where is the next tube station?"

"I´m not sure. Let's ask the nice guard."

They (4) ______ (return) to the entrance hall, where the guard still stands, and ask her.

"The closest underground station is Tottenham Court Road," she says, telling them how to get there.

"Thank you," the children reply and (5) ______ (leave) the museum.

When they reach the tube station, they look for a tube map.

"Look," Mary says, pointing at the map. "We are here, and we can take the black line to Charing Cross and then the brown line to Baker Street."

Suddenly, Mycroft starts growling again.

"Sh, Mycroft, quiet! What's the matter with you?" While John is (6) ______ (try) to calm Mycroft down, Mary (7) ______ (look) around.

"Strange, that man with the beard and the sunglasses who was on the bus is (8) ______ (stand) over there and (9) ______ (read) a newspaper! Mycroft really doesn't like him. Wait, isn't that the guy from the antique shop?"

John looks at him. "Mr Milverton from the Sherlock Holmes fan club? But why is he (10) ______ (wear) a **disguise**?"

"I think he is following us to find the manuscript!"

John looks very angry. "I think you are right. Let's try to **mislead** him."

Mycroft is still (11) ______ (growl), but John ignores him and looks at the map again. Very loudly, he says, "There, let's take the black line to Embankment and then the green line to Tower Hill. From there we can walk to the Tower. Let's go."

And they quickly (12) ______ (walk) down the stairs towards the underground trains.

When the next train arrives, John and Mary step inside. They **notice** that the man with the beard also gets on the train a few doors further down. At the last moment, when the doors are closing, the children and Mycroft jump out of the train. The man with the beard looks shocked and angry, but the train is already moving.

They wait for the next train and step inside.

Complete the sentences

Fill in verbs in the present progressive or present simple

(1) Every day, Mary ______ (eats / is eating) muesli in the morning.
(2) My father ______ (washes / is washing) the dishes at the moment.
(3) She ______ (goes / is going) swimming every day.
(4) I usually ________ (get up / am getting up) at 6 o'clock.
(5) My mother often ______ (wears / is wearing) a hat, but she ______ (doesn't wear / is not wearing) a hat today.
(6) We ______ (have / are having) dinner now.

Form questions with the present progressive

Example: *She is riding a bike.* => *Is she riding a bike?*

(1) You are going home.
(2) They are swimming in the sea.
(3) He is living in Berlin.
(4) I am driving a car.
(5) We are taking photos.

(1) ____

(2) ____

(3) ____

(4) ____

(5) ____

Build the negative form

Example:
She is riding a bike. => She is not riding a bike. / She isn't riding a bike.

(1) He is playing the piano.
(2) I am listening.
(3) We are swimming in the sea.
(4) You are writing a letter.
(5) They are cooking dinner.

(1) ______________________________

(2) ______________________________

(3) ______________________________

(4) ______________________________

(5) ______________________________

Translation

DER SELTSAME MANN

„‚*SWW*' klingt unwahrscheinlich“, sagt Mary, „aber was ist mit ‚*SOO*' oder ‚*SUU*?“

Eine alte Frau, die neben den beiden steht, dreht sich zu den Kindern um. „Was redet ihr denn da? Wir sind hier nicht im Zoo. Das ist ein Museum!“

John und Mary lachen laut auf. „Natürlich, der Zoo! Danke vielmals!“

Die ältere Frau schüttelt den Kopf und geht weg.

„Wir müssen also zum Londoner Zoo", sagt John. „Aber wie kommen wir da hin?"

„Ich war letzten Monat mit meinen Eltern im Zoo", sagt Mary. „Ich glaube, wir können mit der U-Bahn bis zur Station Baker Street fahren."

„Na gut, aber wo ist die nächste U-Bahn-Station?"

„Ich bin mir nicht sicher. Fragen wir doch die nette Museumswächterin."

Sie kehren in die Eingangshalle zurück, wo die Wächterin immer noch steht, und fragen sie.

„Die nächstgelegene U-Bahn-Station ist Tottenham Court Road", sagt sie und beschreibt ihnen, wie sie dorthin kommen.

„Danke", antworten die Kinder und verlassen das Museum.

Als sie die U-Bahn-Station erreichen, suchen sie nach einem U-Bahn-Plan.

„Schau", sagt Mary und zeigt auf die Karte. „Wir sind hier und können mit der schwarzen Linie bis Charing Cross und dann mit der braunen Linie bis Baker Street fahren."

Plötzlich fängt Mycroft wieder an zu knurren.

„Pst, Mycroft, ruhig! Was ist denn los mit dir?" Während John versucht, Mycroft zu beruhigen, sieht sich Mary um.

„Komisch, der Mann mit dem Bart und der Sonnenbrille, der im Bus war, steht da drüben und liest eine Zeitung! Mycroft kann ihn wirklich nicht leiden. Warte, ist das nicht der Typ aus dem Antiquitätenladen?"

John sieht ihn an. „Mr. Milverton vom Sherlock-Holmes-Fanclub? Aber warum trägt er eine Verkleidung?"

„Ich glaube er folgt uns, um das Manuskript zu finden!"

John sieht sehr wütend aus. „ Ich denke du hast Recht. Komm, wir versuchen, ihn in die Irre zu führen."

Mycroft knurrt immer noch, aber John ignoriert ihn und sieht wieder auf die Karte. Dann sagt er sehr laut: „Da, wir nehmen die schwarze Linie zum Embankment und dann die grüne Linie zum Tower Hill. Von dort aus können wir zum Tower laufen. Auf geht‘s.“

Und sie gehen schnell die Treppe hinunter zu den U-Bahn-Zügen.

Als der nächste Zug ankommt, steigen John und Mary ein. Sie bemerken, dass der Mann mit dem Bart ein paar Türen weiter ebenfalls in den Zug einsteigt. Im letzten Moment, als sich die Türen schließen, springen die Kinder und Mycroft aus dem Zug. Der Mann mit dem Bart sieht schockiert und wütend aus, aber der Zug fährt bereits ab.

Sie warten auf den nächsten Zug und steigen ein.

11 | THE LAST CLUE

Simple past

"That was close!" Mary says when they sit down on the underground train. "We have to be careful with this man."

"You're right," John says. He shakes his head. "I never thought that Mr Milverton would try to do this!"

"Well, we **got rid** of him, so don't worry about him. What is the next clue from the letter?"

John takes out the piece of paper. "Conan Doyle wrote '*kauri 4* ***yards*** *up*'."

"I understand what a yard is," Mary says, "but what is a kauri?"

"I have no idea. Perhaps an animal, since we are going to the zoo? But if it lived in Conan Doyle's time, it is **dead** now. Let's ask a **zookeeper**. They know about all the animals."

The children get out at Baker Street station. In the street, John points to a large statue. "Look, that's Sherlock Holmes! In the stories, he lived here at 221B Baker Street."

"Great, but did you see a sign for the zoo?"

"No, I didn't."

They look around. "Over there!" Mary says, and they walk down the street.

When they come to the zoo, they look for a zookeeper. After a while, they see one at the tiger **compound**.

"Excuse me," John says, "we are searching for a 'kauri'. Is that an animal? We think it lived in the zoo in 1929."

The zookeeper laughs. "No, it didn't. A kauri is not an animal but a tree. It **grows** in Australia and in New Zealand."

"Oh," says Mary, "is there a kauri tree in the zoo?"

"Yes, there is. **Queen Victoria** planted it more than 150 years ago. It is behind the **porcupine** compound. You can't **miss** it. It's very tall."

"Thank you very much."

They go to the porcupine compound and see a tall, thick tree behind it. "That must be it!" Mary says. "Do you think the clue '*4 yards up*' means we have to climb the tree?"

"Yes, I think so."

They look up the **trunk**. "Look, there is a **knothole** about 4 yards up!" John cries excitedly. "Perhaps Conan Doyle **hid** the last clue inside the hole."

Unfortunately, the lower part of the trunk has no **branches**.

"We need a **ladder**!" John says, looking around. "Over there is a **shed**. Let's go and look."

Inside the shed, they find a **wheelbarrow** and a ladder.

"I just hope no one is watching," Mary says.

She looks outside to see if **the coast is clear**, and then they **carry** the ladder to the tree.

"I'll go," Mary says and climbs up the ladder. "There's something in the knothole! I have it!"

Mary slowly climbs down and holds out a small **plate** to John. It is **made of metal** and very dirty.

"There is text underneath the dirt." Mary **wipes** away the dirt and reads:

> *Well done, you found the last clue! The manuscript is in the* ***British Library****.*

Vocabulary

Englisch	Deutsch
to get rid of s.b./s.th.	jemanden/etwas loswerden
yard	britisches Längenmaß (1 yard = ca. 91 cm)
to be dead	tot sein
the zookeeper	der Zoowärter, Tierpfleger
the compound	das Gehege
to grow	wachsen
Queen Victoria	Queen Victoria war die Britische Königin von 1837 bis 1901.
the porcupine	das Stachelschwein
to miss	übersehen
the trunk	der Baumstamm
the knothole	das Astloch
hid	Vergangenheit von to hide: verstecken
unfortunately	unglücklicherweise, leider
the branch	der Ast
the ladder	die Leiter
the shed	der Schuppen
the wheelbarrow	die Schubkarre
The coast is clear.	Die Luft ist rein.
to carry	tragen
the plate	das Schild, die Tafel

made of metal	aus Metall sein
to wipe	wischen
the library; the British Library	die Bibliothek; Die British Library ist die Nationalbibliothek Großbritanniens und mit 170-200 Millionen Werken eine der größten Bibliotheken der Welt.

Gap text 1: Simple past

Fill in verbs in the simple past

"That (1) ______ (is) close!" Mary says when they sit down on the underground train. "We have to be careful with this man."

"You're right," John says. He shakes his head. "I never (2) ______ (think) that Mr Milverton would try to do this!"

"Well, we (3) ______ **(get) rid** of him, so don't worry about him. What is the next clue from the letter?"

John takes out the piece of paper. "Conan Doyle (4) ______ (write) '*kauri 4* ***yards*** *up*'."

"I understand what a yard is," Mary says, "but what is a kauri?"

"I have no idea. Perhaps an animal, since we are going to the zoo? But if it (5) ______ (live) in Conan Doyle's time, it is **dead** now. Let's ask a **zookeeper**. They know about all the animals."

The children get out at Baker Street station. In the street, John points to a large statue. "Look, that's Sherlock Holmes! In the stories, he (6) ______ (live) here at 221B Baker Street."

"Great, but (7) ______ (do) you see a sign for the zoo?"

"No, I (8) ______ (do not)."

They look around. "Over there!" Mary says, and they walk down the street.

When they come to the zoo, they look for a zookeeper. After a while, they see one at the tiger **compound**.

"Excuse me," John says, "we are searching for a 'kauri'. Is that an animal? We think it (9) ______ (live) in the zoo in 1929."

The zookeeper laughs. "No, it (10) ______ (do not). A kauri is not an animal but a tree. It **grows** in Australia and in New Zealand."

"Oh," says Mary, "is there a kauri tree in the zoo?"

"Yes, there is. Queen Victoria (11) ______ (plant) it more than 150 years ago. It is behind the **porcupine** compound. You can't **miss** it. It's very tall."

"Thank you very much."

They go to the porcupine compound and see a tall, thick tree behind it. "That must be it!" Mary says. "Do you think the clue '*4 yards up*' means we have to climb the tree?"

"Yes, I think so."

They look up the **trunk**. "Look, there is a **knothole** about 4 yards up!" John cries excitedly. "Perhaps Conan Doyle (12) ______ (**hide**) the last clue inside the hole."

Unfortunately, the lower part of the trunk has no **branches**.

"We need a **ladder**!" John says, looking around. "Over there is a **shed**. Let's go and look."

Inside the shed, they find a **wheelbarrow** and a ladder.

"I just hope no one is watching," Mary says.

She looks outside to see if **the coast is clear**, and then they carry the ladder to the tree.

"I'll go," Mary says and climbs up the ladder. "There's something in the knothole! I have it!"

Mary slowly climbs down and holds out a small **plate** to John. It is **made of metal** and very dirty.

"There is text underneath the dirt." Mary **wipes** away the dirt and reads:

> *Well done, you (13) ______ (find) the last clue! The manuscript is in the* ***British Library***.

Bring the words into the correct order

1)	from	What is	the letter	the next	clue
2)	zookeeper	Let's	a	ask	
3)	hid	Conan Doyle	clue	inside the hole	the last

(1) ______________________________

(2) ______________________________

(3) ______________________________

Answer the questions about the story

(1) Why is there a statue of Sherlock Holmes in Baker Street?
(2) Where do the children find a zookeeper?
(3) What is a kauri?
(4) Who planted the kauri tree more than 150 years ago?
(5) What do the children find in the shed?

(1) ______________________________

(2) ______________________________

(3) ______________________________

(4) ______________________________

(5) ______________________________

Translation
DER LETZTE HINWEIS

„Das war knapp!“ sagt Mary, als sie sich in der U-Bahn hinsetzen. „Wir müssen uns vor diesem Mann in Acht nehmen.“

„Du hast Recht“, sagt John. Er schüttelt den Kopf. „Ich hätte nie gedacht, dass Mr. Milverton so etwas versuchen würde!“

„Nun, wir sind ihn losgeworden, also mach dir keine Sorgen um ihn. Was ist der nächste Hinweis aus dem Brief?“

John nimmt das Stück Papier heraus. „Conan Doyle schrieb *‚Kauri 4 Yards oben‘.*“

„Ich weiß, was ein Yard ist“, sagt Mary, „aber was ist ein Kauri?“

„Ich habe keine Ahnung. Vielleicht ein Tier, denn wir gehen ja in den Zoo? Aber wenn es zu Conan Doyles Zeiten gelebt hat, ist es jetzt tot. Fragen wir doch einen Zoowärter. Die wissen über alle Tiere Bescheid.“

Die Kinder steigen an der U-Bahn-Station Baker Street aus. Auf der Straße zeigt John auf eine große Statue. „Schau, das ist Sherlock Holmes! In den Geschichten wohnte er hier in der Baker Street 221B.“

„Toll, aber hast du ein Schild für den Zoo gesehen?“

„Nein, habe ich nicht.“

Sie sehen sich um. „Da drüben!“ sagt Mary, und sie gehen die Straße hinunter.

Als sie am Zoo ankommen, suchen sie nach einem Zoowärter. Nach einer Weile sehen sie einen beim Tigergehege.

„Entschuldigen Sie“, sagt John, „wir suchen einen 'Kauri'. Ist das ein Tier? Wir glauben, dass es 1929 im Zoo gelebt hat.“

Der Zoowärter lacht. „Nein, hat es nicht. Ein Kauri ist kein Tier, sondern ein Baum. Er wachst in Australien und in Neuseeland.“

„Oh“, sagt Mary, „gibt es einen Kauri Baum im Zoo?“

„Ja, den gibt es. Königin Victoria hat ihn vor mehr als 150 Jahren gepflanzt. Er steht hinter dem Stachelschweingehege. Du kannst ihn nicht übersehen. Er ist sehr groß.“

„Vielen Dank."

Sie gehen zum Stachelschweingehege und sehen dahinter einen hohen, dicken Baum. „Das muss er sein!" sagt Mary. „Meinst du, der Hinweis ‚*4 Yards oben*' bedeutet, dass wir auf den Baum klettern müssen?"

„Ja, ich glaube schon."

Sie sehen den Baumstamm hinauf. „Schau, da ist ein Astloch in ungefähr 4 Yards Höhe!" ruft John aufgeregt. „Vielleicht hat Conan Doyle den letzten Hinweis in dem Loch versteckt."

Leider hat der untere Teil des Stammes keine Äste.

„Wir brauchen eine Leiter!" sagt John und sieht sich um. „Da drüben ist ein Schuppen. Sehen wir nach."

Im Inneren des Schuppens finden sie eine Schubkarre und eine Leiter.

„Ich hoffe nur, dass niemand uns sieht", sagt Mary.

Sie blickt nach draußen, um zu sehen, ob die Luft rein ist, und dann tragen sie die Leiter zu dem Baum.

„Ich mache es", sagt Mary und klettert die Leiter hinauf. „Da ist etwas im Astloch! Ich habe es!"

Mary klettert langsam hinunter und hält John ein kleines Schild hin. Es ist aus Metall und sehr schmutzig.

„Unter dem Schmutz steht ein Text." Mary wischt den Schmutz weg und liest:

> *Gut gemacht, Sie haben den letzten Hinweis gefunden! Das Manuskript befindet sich in der British Library.*

12 | MISSION IMPOSSIBLE

Mixed bag

Mary and John walk back to the tube station and take the train to King's Cross.

"What is the last clue from the letter?" Mary asks when they leave the tube and walk to the library.

John takes out the paper. "It's '*YC.1929.S.25*'."

"That could be a **shelfmark**," Mary says. "That's the number at the side of a library book so that it can be found on the **shelves**."

"How does it work?"

"We have to find the shelf with all the 'YC' books on it. Then, look for books with '1929' and 'S'. When we find these books, there should be one book with the number 25. And that is the book we want."

When they come to the library, they look around. There are many people, but the children can't see any books. Luckily, there's an information desk.

"Excuse me," John asks the woman who is sitting there. "Where are all the books?"

"You must **order** them online," the woman explains. "But **perhaps** I can help you?"

"We are looking for a specific book," Mary says. "The shelfmark is YC.1929.S.25."

The woman **types** into her computer. "That's *The Sign of the Five* by Dean Colony."

"Can we **borrow** it?"

"No, I'm sorry. It's a very **rare** book and cannot be borrowed."

The children look at **each other** in shock.

"But you have it here?" Mary asks.

"Yes, down in the **basement**."

"Thank you," John says and pulls Mary away.

"What do we do now?" Mary asks.

They both think hard. Suddenly, Mycroft starts growling again. Mary and John look up and see Mr Milverton standing beside them. He quickly grabs Mary's arm and presses something into her back.

"I have a gun; don't say a word and **calm** your dog **down**," he **hisses**.

John **obeys** but stares angrily at Mr Milverton.

"I know you have the shelfmark," Mr Milverton whispers. "Where can we find the book?"

"It's down in the basement," John says, "but we **are** not **allowed to** go there."

Mr Milverton looks around, then pulls Mary to the next wall with him. There is a **fire alarm button**, and when no one is looking, he presses it. The fire alarm sounds, and everyone starts leaving the building.

"Down there," Mr Milverton says when the entrance hall is empty, and pulls Mary towards the stairs. John and Mycroft follow.

The basement is empty, too. It is **huge**, with thousands of shelves and millions of books.

"Show me the shelfmark!" Mr Milverton says.

John shows him.

"YC.1929.S.25." Mr Milverton looks around. "'YC', that's over there," and he walks towards the shelf.

They search until they find the books with the numbers 1929. Then they look for S and then for 25. Finally, they find *The Sign of the Five.*

"There it is," Mr Milverton says triumphantly, **reaching for** the book.

At that moment, John sees that Mr Milverton has no real gun, only a water pistol.

"Attack!" John tells Mycroft. "Run, Mary, he hasn't got a gun!"

Mr Milverton **startles**, Mary quickly takes the book from his hands, and she and John run for the exit. They hear Mycroft barking and Mr Milverton shouting behind them.

When they arrive in the entrance hall, Mycroft **catches up** with them again. But Mr Milverton is nowhere to be seen.

Mary and John run out of the library. There are fire engines and police cars in front of the building, and the children immediately go to a police officer.

"Please, we have to tell you something," John **pants**.

They tell the police officer everything, and he goes into the library to check for Mr Milverton.

"Let's look at the book," Mary says. They sit on a nearby bench and slowly, Mary opens the book. They're surprised to find a large **hole** in the middle, and inside it, they find a thick **package** with many pages. On the top page, they read:

> *Congratulations, you found my manuscript! I hope you enjoyed the* **treasure hunt**, *and I hope you enjoy my last story.*
> *Conan Doyle.*

Vocabulary

Englisch	Deutsch
the shelfmark	die Signatur
the shelf (Pl. shelves)	das Regal, das Regalbrett
to order	bestellen
perhaps	vielleicht
to type	tippen, schreiben
to borrow	(sich) ausleihen
rare	selten
each other	einander, gegenseitig
the basement	der Keller, das Untergeschoss
to calm down	sich/jmd. beruhigen
to hiss	zischen
to obey	gehorchen
to be allowed to do s.th.	etwas tun dürfen
the fire alarm button	der Feueralarmknopf
huge	riesengroß
to reach for	nach etwas greifen
to startle	erschrecken
to catch up	einholen
to pant	keuchen
the hole	das Loch
the package	das Paket
the treasure hunt	die Schnitzeljagd

Gap text 1: Mixed bag

Fill in the missing words

Mary and John walk back to the tube station and take the train to King's Cross.

"(1) ______ (What / Why / How) is the last clue from the letter?" Mary asks when they leave the tube and walk to the library.

John (2) ______ (take) out the paper. "It's '*YC.1929.S.25*'."

"That could be a **shelfmark**," Mary says. "That's the number at the side of a library book so that it can be found on the **shelves**."

"(3) ______ (Where / Why / How) does it work?"

"We have to find the shelf with all the 'YC' books on it. Then, look for books with '1929' and 'S'. When we find these books, there should be one book with the number 25. And that is the book we (4) ______ (want)."

When they come to the library, they look around. There are many people, but the children can't see any books. Luckily, there's an information desk.

"Excuse me," John (5) ______ (ask) the woman who is sitting there. "(6) ______ (Where / What / How) are all the books?"

"You must **order** them online," the woman explains. "But **perhaps** I can help you?"

"We are (7) ______ (look) for a specific book," Mary says. "The shelfmark is YC.1929.S.25."

The woman **types** into her computer. "(8) ______ (That's / These are) *The Sign of the Five* by Dean Colony."

"Can we **borrow** it?"

"No, I'm sorry. It's a very **rare** book and (9) ______ (can / cannot / must) be borrowed."

The children look at **each other** in shock.

"But you have it here?" Mary asks.

"Yes, down in the **basement**."

"Thank you," John says and pulls Mary away.

"What do we do now?" Mary asks.

They both think hard. Suddenly, Mycroft starts growling again. Mary and John look up and see Mr Milverton standing beside them. He quickly grabs Mary's arm and presses something into her back.

"I have a gun; don't say a word and **calm** your dog **down**," he **hisses**.

John **obeys** but stares angrily at Mr Milverton.

"I (10) ______ (know) you have the shelfmark," Mr Milverton whispers. "Where can we find the book?"

"It's down in the basement," John says, "but we **are** not **allowed to** go there."

Mr Milverton looks around, then (11) ______ (pull) Mary to the next wall with him. There is a fire alarm **button**, and when no one is looking, he presses it. The fire alarm sounds, and everyone starts leaving the building.

"Down there," Mr Milverton says when the entrance hall is empty, and pulls Mary towards the stairs. John and Mycroft follow.

The basement is empty, too. (12) ______ (It is / They are) **huge**, with thousands of shelves and millions of books.

"Show me the shelfmark!" Mr Milverton says.

John shows him.

"YC.1929.S.25." Mr Milverton looks around. "'YC', that's over there," and he walks towards the shelf.

They search until they find the books with the numbers 1929. Then they look for S and then for 25. Finally, they find *The Sign of the Five*.

"There it is," Mr Milverton says triumphantly, **reaching for** the book.

At that moment, John sees that Mr Milverton has no real gun, only a water pistol.

"Attack!" John tells Mycroft. "Run, Mary, he (13) ______ (hasn't got / haven't got) a gun!"

Mr Milverton **startles**, Mary quickly takes the book from his hands, and she and John run for the exit. They hear Mycroft barking and Mr Milverton shouting behind them.

When they arrive in the entrance hall, Mycroft **catches up** with them again. But Mr Milverton is nowhere to be seen.

Mary and John run out of the library. There are fire engines and police cars in front of the building, and the children immediately go to a police officer.

"Please, we have to tell you something," John **pants**.

They tell the police officer everything, and he goes into the library to check for Mr Milverton.

"Let's look at the book," Mary says. They sit on a nearby bench and slowly, Mary opens the book. They're surprised to find a large **hole** in the middle, and inside it, they find a thick **package** with many pages. On the top page, they read:

> *Congratulations, you (14) ______ (find) my manuscript! I hope you (15) ______ (enjoy) the* ***treasure hunt****, and I hope you enjoy my last story.*
>
> *Conan Doyle.*

Fill in the missing words

(1) A ______ is the number at the side of a library book so that it can be found on the shelves.
(2) Books at the British library must be ordered ____.
(3) Mr Milverton presses a ______ into Mary's back.
(4) Everyone leaves the library because of the ____.

Match the words with the correct translation

(1) library	a) erklären
(2) information desk	b) leer
(3) to explain	c) Bibliothek, Bücherei
(4) back	d) bellen
(5) empty	e) Informationsschalter
(6) to bark	f) Rücken

Translation

MISSION IMPOSSIBLE

Mary und John gehen zurück zur U-Bahn-Station und nehmen den Zug nach King's Cross.

„Was ist der letzte Hinweis aus dem Brief?" fragt Mary, als sie die U-Bahn verlassen und zur Bibliothek gehen.

John nimmt das Blatt heraus. „Es ist ‚*YC.1929.S.25*'."

„Das könnte eine Signatur sein", sagt Mary. „Das ist die Nummer an der Seite eines Bibliotheksbuchs, damit es in den Regalen gefunden werden kann."

„Wie funktioniert das?"

„Wir müssen das Regal finden, in dem alle ‚YC'-Bücher stehen. Dann suchen wir nach Büchern mit ‚1929' und ‚S'. Wenn wir diese Bücher gefunden haben, sollte es ein Buch mit der Nummer 25 geben. Und das ist das Buch, das wir wollen."

Als sie in die Bibliothek kommen, schauen sie sich um. Die Kinder können viele Menschen sehen, aber keine Bücher. Zum Glück gibt es einen Informationsschalter.

„Entschuldigen Sie", fragt John die Frau, die dort sitzt. „Wo sind die Bücher?"

„Ihr müsst sie online bestellen", erklärt die Frau. „Aber vielleicht kann ich euch helfen?"

„Wir suchen ein bestimmtes Buch", sagt Mary. „Die Signatur lautet YC.1929.S.25."

Die Frau tippt in ihren Computer. „Das ist *Das Zeichen der Fünf* von Dean Colony."

„Können wir es ausleihen?"

„Nein, es tut mir leid. Es ist ein sehr seltenes Buch und kann nicht ausgeliehen werden."

Die Kinder sehen sich erschrocken an.

„Aber Sie haben es hier?" fragt Mary.

„Ja, unten im Keller."

„Danke", sagt John und zieht Mary weg.

„Und was machen wir jetzt?" fragt Mary.

Sie denken beide angestrengt nach. Plötzlich fängt Mycroft wieder an zu knurren. Mary und John blicken auf und sehen Mr. Milverton direkt neben sich stehen. Er ergreift schnell Marys Arm und drückt ihr etwas in den Rücken.

„Ich habe eine Waffe; sagt kein Wort und beruhigt euren Hund", zischt er.

John gehorcht, starrt aber wütend auf Mr. Milverton.

„Ich weiß, dass ihr die Signatur habt", flüstert Mr. Milverton. „Wo können wir das Buch finden?"

„Es ist unten im Keller", sagt John, „aber da dürfen wir nicht hin."

Mr. Milverton sieht sich um und zieht Mary mit sich zur nächsten Wand. Dort gibt es einen Feueralarmknopf, und als niemand hinsieht, drückt er ihn. Der Feueralarm ertönt, und alle beginnen, das Gebäude zu verlassen.

„Nach unten", sagt Mr. Milverton, als die Eingangshalle leer ist, und zieht Mary zur Treppe. John und Mycroft folgen ihm.

Auch der Keller ist leer. Er ist riesig, mit Tausenden von Regalen und Millionen von Büchern.

„Zeig mir die Signatur!" sagt Mr. Milverton.

John zeigt sie ihm.

„YC.1929.S.25." Mr. Milverton sieht sich um. „‚YC', das ist dort drüben", und er geht auf das Regal zu.

Sie suchen, bis sie die Bücher mit der Nummer 1929 finden. Dann suchen sie nach S und dann nach 25. Schließlich finden sie *Das Zeichen der Fünf*.

„Da ist es", sagt Mr. Milverton triumphierend und greift nach dem Buch.

In diesem Moment sieht John, dass Mr. Milverton keine richtige Waffe hat, sondern nur eine Wasserpistole.

„Fass!" befielt John Mycroft. „Lauf, Mary, er hat keine Waffe!"

Mr. Milverton erschrickt, Mary nimmt ihm schnell das Buch aus der Hand, und sie und John rennen zum Ausgang. Hinter ihnen hören sie Mycroft bellen und Mr. Milverton schreien.

Als sie in der Eingangshalle ankommen, holt Mycroft sie wieder ein. Aber Mr. Milverton ist nirgends zu sehen.

Mary und John rennen aus der Bibliothek. Vor dem Gebäude stehen Feuerwehrautos und Polizeiautos, und die Kinder gehen sofort zu einem Polizeibeamten.

„Bitte, wir müssen Ihnen etwas sagen", keucht John.

Sie erzählen dem Polizisten alles, und er geht in die Bibliothek, um nach Mr. Milverton zu suchen.

„Sehen wir uns das Buch an", sagt Mary. Sie setzen sich auf eine Bank in der Nähe und Mary schlägt das Buch langsam auf. Zu ihrer Überraschung finden sie in der Mitte ein großes Loch und darin ein dickes Paket mit vielen Seiten. Auf der obersten Seite lesen sie:

> *Glückwunsch, Sie haben mein Manuskript gefunden! Ich hoffe, Sie hatten Spaß bei der Schatzsuche, und ich hoffe, Ihnen gefällt meine letzte Geschichte.*
>
> *Conan Doyle.*

SOLUTIONS – LÖSUNGEN

01 | Mary meets John

Gap text 1: Personal pronouns

(1) She; (2) She; (3) you; (4) She; (5) you; (6) We; (7) you; (8) he; (9) they; (10) He; (11) I; (12) you; (13) we

Gap text 2: Forms of to be

(1) is; (2) Are; (3) is; (4) are / we're; (5) are; (6) am / I'm; (7) is / he's

Answer the questions about the story

(1) Mary is 11 years old.; (2) Mary lives in London.; (3) She meets the dog in the park, after crossing a bridge over a small creek.; (4) She finds the phone number on a pendant at the dog's collar.; (5) She can't phone the owner because she doesn't have a mobile phone.; (6) The dog's name is Mycroft.

02 | At the flea market

Gap text 1: Possessive forms

(1) of; (2) John's; (3) of; (4) of; (5) of; (6) of; (7) Holmes's; (8) Doyle's

Gap text 2: Possessive adjectives

(1) Their; (2) their; (3) her; (4) my; (5) your; (6) his; (7) his; (8) my

Complete the sentences

(1) his; (2) my; (3) our; (4) your; (5) her; (6) their; (7) its

03 | The lost manuscript

Gap text 1: Singular/plural forms and articles

(1) an; (2) books; (3) the; (4) a; (5) the; (6) clues; (7) clue; (8) manuscript; (9) the; (10) a; (11) an; (12) the

Fill in the missing words
(1) house; (2) letter; (3) story

Answer the questions about the story
(1) Mary and John can find the manuscript by following the clues.; (2) It's the prime meridian at the Royal Observatory in Greenwich.; (3) Mary finds out what the first clue means. She knows about the prime meridian.; (4) Charles Dickens is the author of *A Christmas Carol.*

04 | A big mistake

Gap text 1: Have got and haven't got
(1) has got; (2) have you got; (3) haven't got; (4) have got; (5) have you got; (6) have got

Complete the sentences
(1) has got; (2) hasn't got; (3) have got

Build questions with have got/has got
(1) Have we got a car?; (2) Have you got a pencil?; (3) Have I got a cat?; (4) Have they got two sons?; (5) Has he got a red bike?

Match the words with the correct translation
1c; 2d; 3f; 4a; 5b; 6e

05 | At the royal observatory

Gap text 1: Demonstrative pronouns
(1) that; (2) this; (3) this; (4) those; (5) these; (6) those

Complete the sentences
(1) this; (2) that; (3) these those; (4) these; (5) that; (6) those these

Find the words

M	S	T	A	B	O	V	W	Q	**F**
U	A	**S**	**T**	**R**	**A**	**N**	**G**	**E**	**A**
S	L	**N**	**O**	**T**	**E**	**B**	**O**	**O**	**K**
E	M	**N**	**U**	**M**	**B**	**E**	**R**	**S**	**E**
U	S	N	W	**S**	B	V	C	L	O
M	R	P	**W**	C	**C**	K	W	I	K
I	**T**	**O**	**M**	**O**	**R**	**R**	**O**	**W**	S
G	E	H	N	Z	**O**	L	**I**	E	R
J	S	V	W	H	E	**D**	S	**P**	C
H	L	**C**	**L**	**O**	**C**	**K**	E	I	**T**

06 | Mycroft's adventure

Gap text 1: Can and must

(1) must; (2) cannot / can't; (3) mustn't; (4) must; (5) cannot / can't; (6) must; (7) cannot / can't; (8) must; (9) cannot / can't; (10) can; (11) can; (12) mustn't; (13) must

Answer the questions about the story

(1) He is bored because he is tied to a bench and cannot do anything interesting.; (2) He runs away because he sees a squirrel.; (3) The dog Sherlock finds Mycroft and helps him.; (4) Sherlock is a black and white border collie.

Build questions with must and can

(1) Must we go shopping today?; (2) Can I see my friend?; (3) Can you ride a bike?; (4) Must she do her homework?; (5) Can they dance?

07 | In Westminster Abbey

Gap text 1: Do and does

(1) do; (2) does; (3) do not / don't; (4) do; (5) does; (6) does; (7) do not / don't; (8) do not / don't; (9) does; (10) doesn't

Bring the words into the correct order

1) Do you know what that means?; 2) I know this from school.; 3) John searches through the apps on his mobile.; 4) John takes out the piece of paper.; 5) They go on until they are finished.

Answer the questions about the story

(1) No, he doesn't / does not.; (2) Yes, it does.; (3) Yes, they do.; (4) Yes, he does. He's buried there.; (5) Yes, they do.

08 | Taking the bus

Gap text 1: Question words

(1) What; (2) How; (3) what; (4) who; (5) When; (6) Why (7) How; (8) where; (9) Where; (10) What; (11) how

Form questions with question words

(1) Where is the Rosetta Stone?; (2) What is the Rosetta Stone?; (3) Who deciphered the hieroglyphs?; (4) How long does it take to walk to the museum?; (5) Why does John know about Jean-François Champollion?; (6) When did Jean-François Champollion decipher the hieroglyphs?

Match the words with the correct translation

1e; 2f; 3d; 4b; 5c; 6a

09 | At the British Museum

Gap text 1: Present simple

(1) see; (2) looks; (3) says; (4) smiles; (5) see; (6) does; (7) look; (8) see; (9) says; (10) go; (11) does; (12) shakes

Complete the sentences

(1) eats; (2) washes; (3) Does; (4) tries; (5) plays; (6) relaxes; (7) says

10 | The strange man

Gap text 1: Present progressive and present simple

(1) standing; (2) talking; (3) walks; (4) return; (5) leave; (6) trying; (7) looks; (8) standing; (9) reading; (10) wearing; (11) growling; (12) walk

Complete the sentences

(1) eats; (2) is washing; (3) goes; (4) get up; (5) wears is not wearing; (6) are having

Form questions with the present progressive

(1) Are you going home?; (2) Are they swimming in the sea?; (3) Is he living in Berlin?; (4) Am I driving a car?; (5) Are we taking photos?

Build the negative form

(1) He is not playing the piano. / He isn't playing the piano.; (2) I am not listening. / I'm not listening.; (3) We are not swimming in the sea. / We aren't swimming in the sea.; (4) You are not writing a letter. / You aren't writing a letter.; (5) They are not cooking dinner. / They aren't cooking dinner.

11 | The last clue

Gap text 1: Simple past

(1) was; (2) thought; (3) got; (4) wrote; (5) lived; (6) lived; (7) did; (8) didn't / did not; (9) lived; (10) didn't / did not; (11) planted; (12) hid; (13) found

Bring the words into the correct order

1) What is the next clue from the letter?"; 2) Let's ask a zookeeper.; 3) Conan Doyle hid the last clue inside the hole.

Answer the questions about the story

(1) There is a statue of Sherlock Holmes in Baker Street because that is where he lived in the stories.; (2) They find a zookeeper at the tiger compound.; (3) It's a tree that grows in Australia and New Zealand.; (4) Queen Victoria planted it.; (5) In the shed they find a wheelbarrow and a ladder.

12 | Mission impossible

Gap text 1: Mixed bag

(1) What; (2) takes; (3) How; (4) want; (5) asks; (6) Where; (7) looking; (8) That's; (9) cannot; (10) know; (11) pulls; (12) It is; (13) hasn't got; (14) found; (15) enjoyed

Fill in the missing words

(1) shelfmark; (2) online; (3) gun /water pistol; (4) fire alarm

Match the words with the correct translation

1c; 2e; 3a; 4f; 5b; 6d

NACHWORT – EPILOGUE

Liebe Leserin, lieber Leser,

ich hoffe, dass du Spaß beim Lesen, Anhören und Mitraten hattest! Wenn du alle Kapitel gelesen/gehört und alle Übungen gemacht hast, bist du gut für die 6. Klasse gerüstet. Vielleicht gibt es auch bald neue Abenteuer mit Mary und John – ich würde mich freuen, wenn du dann wieder dabei bist.

Viele Grüße,

Stefanie Fricke

FEEDBACK

Falls du oder deine Eltern Fragen oder Anregungen habt oder Feedback geben möchtet, freuen wir uns über eine E-Mail an info@ehrengut-verlag.de. Wir schätzen jede einzelne E-Mail und werden uns so schnell wie möglich bei euch zurückmelden.

Möchtest du unseren Verlag unterstützen?

Dann freuen wir uns über deine Online-Rezension.
Vielen Dank!

Thank you!

Zeitfracht Medien GmbH
Ferdinand-Jühlke-Straße 7
99095 Erfurt, Deutschland
produktsicherheit@kolibri360.de